BUILDING A WRITING LIFE

Hillary DePiano

HillaryDePiano.com

TABLE OF CONTENTS

INTRODUCTION

You want to be a writer. It's something you've thought about a lot but still aren't sure how to make happen. What marks the difference between occasional scribbling and the writing life?

"Writers write!" people say, but what the heck does that mean? If it were that easy to shed your aspiring status and emerge tomorrow as an honest to goodness writer, you'd have done that already! One of the most frustrating things about being a creative is how so much advice is generalized to the point of vague hand-waving when all you want is a straight answer on exactly what you need to do to get where you want to be.

This book is that straight answer. It's a straightforward, step-by-step plan. A simple collection of actionable steps you can start taking right now that will take you on the path to becoming a writer.

To building a writing life.

What this isn't is a guide to writing the next bestseller or how to master any particular writing form or genre. It's not about publication or marketing or how to profit from your writing. It's about getting started with building up a regular writing habit and integrating writing into your life so you can achieve your goals.

In my role as a volunteer with NaNoWriMo, I talk to a lot of first-time writers, and so many of them talk about writing as if it were a flight of stairs. As if they only need to climb a little more and then they'll stand, triumphant, on the landing forevermore. But that magic landing does not exist.

I have never met a writer that only has one story to tell. Perhaps there is a person out there with exactly one thing to write, and then nothing else to say for the rest of their lives but all I have met instead are people bursting with words and worlds and stories, a whole lifetime of them. For them, writing is not a single destination but the journey of a lifetime.

No, a writing life is not a flight of stairs. It's not a fancy bed-and-breakfast you visit once in a while or a warehouse churning out boxes of books. It's a house. A home. Something stable and comfortable where you can live out the rest of your creative life. It's an everyday space: utility enough that you can make your way around in the dark by habit alone but where you can still find the wonder of that perfect morning sun through the kitchen window. A safe place in your head where dreams can flourish and words can flow.

This book is about building that writing life. And, no, it does not matter what you are writing. Memoir, non-fiction, articles, novels, scripts... you can do whatever you want in the privacy of your own home, after all. Whether you are just looking to write for yourself or have more commercial goals, you still must build space for writing in your life. So let's make that space together.

I've organized this book into four sections to help you think about building your writing life in the same way as building a house.

These are:

Secure Your Contractors
Make the Mental Commitment

Break Ground
Start Writing

Build a Solid Foundation
Establish a Regular Writing Habit

Move In
Discover Your Writing Process

Before we start this journey together, a quick introduction. I'm a playwright, fiction and non-fiction author of over three dozen books and plays over several pen names and, though I knew I wanted to be a writer since I was a little kid, I didn't build myself a proper writing life until about a decade ago. I went from being someone overflowing with ideas that only wrote a few pages a year to someone writing regularly and growing a professional writing career despite an overbooked life.

Which is all to say that I have been where you are, wanting so badly to integrate more writing into my life but with no idea how to get started. So let me save you the years of floundering and failure and wasted time I had to go through until I finally figured it out. Let's build you a writing habit strong enough to withstand whatever life throws at it.

SECURE YOUR CONTRACTORS

Make the Mental Commitment

You wouldn't start to build a house unless you knew everyone on the project was completely on board. Contacts in place, everything all agreed upon in black and white, permits filed and approved. If you've ever been part of a big construction project, you know that just one contractor on the wrong page can derail the whole project and turn a dream house into a nightmare.

When it comes to building your writing life, there's a chorus of voices in your head, and the first step to doing this thing is to get them all committed. That means it's time to get your mental paperwork in order. It may sound silly but, the fact is, if your mental team were already 100% on board with this writing thing, you wouldn't be reading this book you'd be doing it.

Getting your head around the conceptual part of being a writer is the most important part and the most often overlooked. It's also not easy. The good news is the fact that you are reading this means you've already cleared the very first hurdle most aspiring writers never even make it past.

Consider how many people, and you might know a few in your immediate circle of friends and family, dream of writing but have never taken even a single step towards making that fantasy into reality. But you, you're here! And that means you've already taken that all-important first step.

It's very easy to underestimate what a big deal that is.

So take a moment to congratulate yourself! You've already made an important mental commitment to becoming a writer, and that's a big something.

Now, let's talk about what else you need to do.

> **In this section,** you'll claim the title of writer and give yourself permission to write, even if it's badly. You'll make writing a priority in your life, clarify your writing purpose, and solidify your determination tangibly. You'll transform your writing dreams into a writing goal and discover that the magic of writing is in you, not in writing tricks and gimmicks. You'll start building your writing tribe by acting like the professional writer you aren't yet without getting distracted by comparisons and petty jealousy. You'll level up your writing skills and broaden your writing perspective by reading widely and often and, most importantly, truly commit to your goals by taking failure entirely off the table.

Join me, as we machete our way past fears, doubts, hang-ups, and hesitation to the place where your determination lives. Now it's time to get mentally prepared, and that starts when you claim your rightful title as a writer.

Call yourself a writer

Do you feel comfortable calling yourself a writer? One of the most common mental hang-ups I've seen in beginning writers is this reluctance to call themselves a writer... "yet." There's always some arbitrary benchmark they've set up in their head for when they'll be worthy of the title, something that designates when they are a Real Writer. Often, this benchmark moves as they progress in their career so it's always just out of their current reach.

But, the thing is, all a writer is is someone who writes. That's it. There's no special certification, approval board or trial by fire. You can call yourself a writer right now, and no one can stop you.

Do you still demur, shying away from using the title? Then you've found the first bit of mental work you've got to do. How are you going to commit to writing if you don't even consider yourself a writer? If you're not even willing to admit it to yourself, how will you defend it to others? How can you justify making room for something in your life that you don't even believe in enough to call by its name?

You are a writer. Write that on a post-it note and put it where you'll see it every day until you believe it. Introduce yourself that way to random strangers. Wear that coat with pride even if it still doesn't quite feel like it fits because the word writer is a magic garment that conforms to fit the wearer as long as you believe.

Give yourself permission to write

Sounds simple, right?

Sometimes it's the hardest thing of all.

There's that pile of laundry, and it's well past time to clean out that fuzzy stuff in the fridge and that birthday party won't plan itself... how can you justify using this time to write when there's all that and more to do?

And even if you get your butt in the chair to write your brain starts up a different list. Your chances of ever getting published are so slim and writing at all is such a silly thing anyway and, really, your story is a mess, and you're not even a very good writer so what's the point? After all, lots of people want to write. Who's to say you're the person who deserves to actually do it?

Stop.

Do you want to write? Then you have permission to write. It's that simple.

Your talents, future prospects, and earning potential have nothing to do with it. You have permission to write if you are awful, if you never make a dime, if you write for yourself and never show it to anyone. The state of your house, work Inbox, and the collection of chaos that totals your personal life all have nothing to do with it either.

It's so easy to play the comparison game, to pit writing against something else in your life and pick a winner (which is seldom writing, it seems). There's always something that feels more important. But if writing is important to you, you have permission to do it.

But you don't need my permission. You need your own.

Can you do that? Can you give yourself permission to write? Can you believe in your right to write enough that you'll carve time out of your day for writing, sacrifice for it, put it above the things that matter to you less? Can you commit to it the way you commit to everything else you've already given yourself permission to make a part of your life?

You can. If this writing thing matters to you, you can and you will.

It might feel awkward at first. There will be moments when you still find yourself overwhelmed by doubts and fear. There are always moments like that in anything worth doing so you may as well get used to them and carry on, anyway.

But things will shift once you have that beautiful moment when everything clicks and you realize that, yes, you CAN do this and you WILL. That you need not wait for anyone's permission to make your dreams happen. Or that no one can stop you but you. It's when you take that deep breath and say, wow, OK, I guess this is happening... and you make it happen.

All because you gave yourself permission.

Let yourself write poorly

I have talked to so many would-be writers whose writing dreams stalled before they had begun and all for the same reason: when they started writing, what they wrote was so bad they just couldn't continue. What if they just weren't good enough to be a writer? What if they were doing it wrong? It stopped them in their tracks and arrested any forward progress they were making on their dreams.

What I tell these writers is the same thing I will say to you: you will write poorly. It is a natural part of the writing life. There is not one of us that vomits forth a perfect bit of writing every time. We refine and revise and rewrite to get to those lovely sentences you see in the finished work, but those words did not start out like that.

We talked in the last section about giving yourself permission to write. Part of that is giving yourself permission to write badly. To clomp your way through that delicate idea, to butcher grammar and string cliches together like a garland, and make an absolute mess of the nicely ordered story in your head. You will write badly, and it's only by writing badly, by getting it down no matter how ugly, that you can move forward with your writing goals and get to the next stage.

Here's the thing about lousy writing: You're an awful judge of it. Most of the time, the writing you thought was the worst of the worst turns out to be just as good as that paragraph that convinced you the Pulitzer was yours. When you look at your writing later, it's never as bad as you thought it was. Time provides precious perspective on our writing. And even if some time off from it proves that it is truly the greatest pile of garbage ever put to the page, you are still better off having written it than not because any progress is better than none.

Get used to writing poorly. Relish in it. Because it means you are a real writer, one who writes even when the words don't flow like magic. And because bad writing means you're still at least making steady progress on your writing goals.

Prioritize writing

Once you've given yourself permission to write, you'll realize that's not enough. Because it's one thing to say, "Yes, I will write!" and another to do it. You've already got a whole life crammed into 24 hours a day, and there are zillions of things vying for your attention. Writing has a lot of competition.

If you're going to add this new element into your life, you must commit to it by making it a priority. Take a minute, and list everything important to you ranked, and figure out where writing fits. And, for your own sake, be honest. No one will look at this but you so you don't get any points for listing what you think you should value over what you really do. If your #1 priority is getting to play The Sims twelve hours a week, own that, and then figure out how to work writing around it.

This can be an illuminating exercise but can also be a bit of a killjoy. A lot of us start something new with this idea that our life will just magically make room for it. Time will somehow free up without too much inconvenience to our nice comfortable routine. But that is rarely the reality.

Adding a new element to your life means cutting something else out, or at least back. It means sacrificing something that also ranks high on your list of priorities. Add in that you probably already feel you never have enough time for the things that matter to you and you'll chafe even more. The happier and more settled you are in the routine you've got now, the more you must fight yourself to change it up. And the lower you placed writing on your list, the harder it will be to get it done.

If you want to do this thing, you've got to make it a priority. That means sacrificing, turning things down, rethinking what matters to you. Writing is important to you, and now it's time to make your list of priorities reflect that.

For now, this is a mental thing. It's about shifting how you think about writing and where it fits in your life. In the fourth section, we'll talk about strategies for finding and also making time to write even if you're already pretty well booked.

Make the commitment real

I have at least a decade of writing failure behind me. Times I set writing goals and failed catastrophically at even coming close to meeting them. Then, one month, everything changed.

I'd given myself a deadline to finish the first draft of a book as part of the NaNoWriMo 30 day writing challenge. I had my outline and my daily target word count, but the one thing I didn't have was any way to make sure this was the time I finally achieved my goal. What could I do to ensure this time differed from all the other times I'd failed? How could I show that I really seriously for real meant it this time when I said I would finish this thing on time?

I decided on a simple thing. I would, at the end of each writing day, post the word count for my draft on my office door. It was a symbolic gesture as only I knew it was there, but it made the whole effort feel real in a way it never had before. There was what I had accomplished so far, right there in black and white, posted for anyone to see.

And something amazing happened. I felt accountable to the little sticky note on the door. Before I realized what was happening, I had written more than I ever had before in only a few days. After all these years of being unable to even come close to meeting my goals, there I was, right on track.

Then, one day, I went to take down yesterday's word count when I noticed a little shocked face drawn in the corner. To my total surprise, my husband had seen the post-its and been checking out my word count every day. At first, I was very embarrassed because it's silly, right? To post the word count for your draft on your door every day?

But then knowing he was looking only added power to the gesture. It pushed me to write more and accelerate toward the end of the project. "He thinks that was an impressive word count? Ha! I'll bet I can write twice that tonight!" "Ugh, I don't feel like writing tonight, but I'm not leaving yesterday's note up there unchanged so let me at least get 1,000 words down before bed." I slapped that note up each day with renewed pride in everything I'd accomplished.

And I did it. After so many years of aimless writing and missed deadlines, I finished an entire book that year for the first time in my life and finished it well before the deadline, a deadline I'd struggled to come even close to for years. I finally got myself a finished draft! But the most important thing I got that month was the understanding that a goal has to feel physical and real before you can achieve it.

Do you want to reach your goal? Make the commitment. Then make it real.

Tell your friends. Shout about it on social media. Make a financial wager. Post a symbol of your goal somewhere. Do whatever it takes to make sure this time is different.

That simple note on my door made me feel accountable to my goal in a tangible way that a mental commitment alone hadn't. Getting yourself mentally committed is more than half the battle, but taking your writing goals out of your headspace and into the physical world is also essential. After all, the real world is where you'll be writing, and no matter how rich an inner life you've built for your story, you've got to bring it out here to achieve the next steps.

Understand why you write

Ask any writer why they write, and you'll get dozens of different answers. Some use it for therapy or meditation. For others, it's a job or side hustle to earn some extra income. Many writers write to share their story or to make sure the world has the stories they needed when they were young. Some writers can't explain why they write, they only know that they must, or life feels wrong and hollow.

Understanding why you write is essential to understand how you write. It defines your writing purpose and guides the steps you take to achieve it. It's the core of your creative impulse and clarifying it now gives you something to refer to whenever you doubt the process or feel you're being led astray.

Certainty in your own motivations can itself be a source of inspiration. When that inevitable moment comes when you are under attack by the doubts and fears every creative person must battle, you will ask yourself why you even bother. And what happens next depends on how certain you are of the answer. Because if you cannot even tell yourself why you write, you'll have quit before you've begun.

Why do you want to write? An answer may spring to mind, but even that is worth examining. Why are you trying to do this?

Try to nail it down enough so answer the question in a single sentence. In the world of theatre, you'd call this your Artistic Statement. It's a guiding principle for your creative life that you can ground yourself with whenever you lose touch with your purpose.

What do you really want out of your writing life?

When I was in college, I wrote and directed a play, _The Love of Three Oranges,_ as part of my honors thesis. After I graduated, I started getting production requests for that play from all over the world. There were dozens of productions over the years, all across the US and across the globe, and every time I talked with the directors or cast of those productions, they always said the same thing. "We love this play! When are you writing another?"

"Oh, no, no, no!" I would say, laughing, "I'm not a playwright!" I had convinced myself that writing novels was the only TRUE writing and, besides, I didn't know how to write a play. And you can see the flaw in this logic right away... that clearly I knew how to write a play if my first effort was this popular, but I couldn't see it. All I knew is that I had dreamed since I was a little kid of telling stories and had always pictured that as writing novels. Writing for the stage had never figured into that plan.

It was decades later when I realized how silly I was being. What I had wanted as a kid, what my dream had always been, was to tell stories. What did it matter if I told those stories through plays instead of novels if that's how people wanted to hear them?

I had gotten so bogged down with one interpretation of my dream I lost sight of the core. And once I realized this, I stopped trying to force my ideas into novel-length works and started letting them become plays to great success. While I may go back to novels again someday, for now, I am perfectly happy because I am doing what I wanted to do. I am getting to tell stories every day for people who want to hear them, even if it's happening on a stage instead of a page.

Sometimes we get very attached to an idea or one way to achieve our goals or dreams, and we lose sight of what it is we actually want. There are a lot of external pressures and biases coming at you about writing and creative work in general. It's surprisingly easy to convince yourself you want one thing because it's what you think you should want when, deep down, it's not what you want at all. Understanding what you want is the key to figuring out how to get it.

What do you really want from your writing? What is your ideal endgame? What is the core of that goal? Once you know that, you'll have it to focus your efforts and give you a road map on the steps it'll take to get there.

Turn dreams into goals

Change your writing dreams into a writing goal

While people often use the terms interchangeably when talking about writing or anything creative, there's a big difference between a dream and a goal. A dream is a fantasy, a mental picture of how we wish it could be. A goal is a tangible thing you can work toward in the real world.

Even the word goal itself changes how you think about it. A dream feels like an ethereal picture in the distance, but a goal is a finish line you can walk toward right now. What would it take to turn your writing dream into a writing goal? Can you turn that daydream of where you want your writing life to go into a list of precisely what you'd need to do to make it a reality?

Dreams are often vague and undefined, but the best goals are as specific as possible. For example, think about having the dream of writing a novel vs. setting a goal to write at least 300 words a day until you have a draft of at least 100,000 words (the typical length for a traditionally published adult novel). By setting a goal, you'd have a specific plan you could act on daily and a simple way of measuring your progress. And, if you stick with it, you'd have a finished first draft of your novel in a year or less. That's the power of getting specific and turning your dreams into goals.

We'll dive into goal setting in greater depth in the third section.

Build your tribe

While we've been talking about getting the voices in your head on board with this whole writing thing, friends and family can help or hinder your writing in a million ways. One of the best things you can do to help your writing life is finding allies and friendly support, and that search starts with the people you already know. When you have people in your life that will support and respect your writing, that's your tribe, and they can be an essential element for building and maintaining your writing life.

Spread the Word

Have you started telling people about your writing yet? You don't have to. Sometimes keeping it secret, especially at the start, can make the process more exciting and help you keep your momentum without outside influences.

But if you are ready to shout about your new writing journey from the rooftops, do it! It's a great way to connect with like-minded peers and expand your creative networks. Letting people can also influence your writing life in other key ways.

Keep you accountable

When you tell people about your writing, they cannot help but ask about it, and that can help keep you committed to your writing goals. The friend that checks in to see how your novel is going, the spouse who asks how your morning writing session went, my kindergartner asking me over breakfast if I figured out how to deal with that dragon scene yet, it all helps keep me motivated and moving forward with my goals. When the people who matter to you know about your writing and are invested in it, that helps you stay invested too.

The motivating power of SHAME

You know what else is very motivating? Shame. The more people you tell about your writing efforts, the more of a fool you'll feel like if you don't follow through with them. Many a night, I only keep writing because I told too many people I was working on this and I'd rather keep writing than face the humiliation I'd feel if I had to admit I gave up.

See also: Spite. You think I can't do it? JUST WATCH ME.

Power of community

Writing can be a solitary activity, but it doesn't need to be. There are a wealth of writing networks online and off from local writing groups to online communities collected under social media hashtags (try #amwriting, #writingcommunity, and #nanowrimo to start) that help you find other writers. Connecting with like-minded writers online and off can be invaluable throughout the writing process for everything from finding beta readers and critique partners to networking your way to publishing opportunities, but it's especially important when you are just starting out.

A writing community can offer support, advice, and cheer-leading to help keep you writing. Having other writers there to bounce ideas off of, share your writing triumphs and commiserate with on the dark days can enrich your writing process from start to finish. And sometimes, just knowing all these other people are out there writing regularly and getting the words down is enough to help you do it too.

Debut the new writing you

Non-writers don't really get the whole writing thing. At best, they get enthusiastic about the wrong things or have an unrealistic idea of how publishing works. At worst, they are dismissive or downright hostile to your creative efforts. Hollywood has warped the writing mystique, and it's often a challenge to get people to understand and respect what you are actually doing vs. what they imagine you are.

The sooner you tell your friends and family about your new commitment to writing, the sooner they will get it and respect both your time and what you are trying to do. It may not happen right away, and you may have a lot of frustrating and discouraging moments ahead, but laying down some ground rules for how you expect them to respect your writing time and goals right at the start can go a long way towards heading some of those issues off before they begin.

Or you may find that your people are immediately and eagerly your ally! Then you'll have someone to help you defend your writing time or otherwise take on other responsibilities. And that is great! You can't underestimate the value of having a support system and cheering section to support you on this journey.

Comparisons and competition

Back in school, what were you told every time you took a test? Eyes on your own paper! And yet, as we test the waters of our writing life, we can't seem to resist taking a peek at what our neighbor is doing.

Your favorite books have been through hundreds of rounds of editing and revision in the hands of professionals. It's ludicrous to compare them to the first draft you just finished. A writer who's been at it longer has built up writing experience and honed skills you can't realistically expect to mirror when you are just starting out. What looks like an overnight success to you is almost always the result of years of hustling behind the scenes. What we call success is often a combination of privilege, connections, and pure luck as much as hard work and talent.

We're all on our own journey and have our own process. Everyone you meet is fighting invisible battles or hiding secret weapons. Most of the time, you don't even realize you're comparing apples to anacondas.

Never measure your success by the accomplishments of others. That way lies misery. Focus on achieving your own goals and ignore the rest.

Jealousy is a natural and human reaction, but it's also counterproductive to the writing life. There are plenty of words to go around, and the world is infinitely hungry for stories. Other writers are not your competition, they're your coworkers. The writing life gets so much easier when you can be genuinely happy for the triumphs of your peers instead of retreating into resentment or bitterness. Celebrate everyone's achievements with them, and they'll be that much more likely to celebrate yours when you get there too.

The only exception to this rule is if you're the type to find a little healthy competition between friends motivating. For example, writing buddies often challenge each other to word wars, bursts of writing where they compete to see who can write the most words in a set duration. If everyone's starting and stopping their writing at the same time, it evens the playing field. A friend with a similar writing speed can also be a great pace car, giving you a challenging but realistic standard to keep up with as you both dash to the end of your writing project together. While it's not for everyone, getting your competitive spirit engaged is a great way to push yourself to get a little extra written when you're stuck or not in the mood.

But driving yourself batty because your friend just got another book deal, and you didn't? That won't do you any good at all. Give your friend a heartfelt high five and then get back to it. Your turn will come.

Write for the job you want

There's an expression that says, "Dress for the job you want, not the job you have," and it applies well to your writing life. Even though you're just starting out, you likely know where you ultimately want to be. You know the writing life you want to have, even though you're not there yet. The key to getting there is to write for that life now.

What is the writing life you want? Let's say you want to be a bestselling author. You want to have dozens of books out, readers clamoring for more. While that may be the farthest thing from your current writing reality, you can write for the job you want by replicating elements of it right now.

What does the writing life of a bestselling author look like? For starters, they are regularly writing and completing books. They have strict deadlines to meet for each stage of the project (pitch, first draft, final draft, etc.) and as soon as they finish one project, they are looking ahead to the next. They are professional, friendly, and supportive of their industry connections, fans, and peers, and they work steadily to grow their careers book by book.

There's no reason you can't do these things right now even though you don't have the big book deals yet. You can be friendly and professional to everyone you meet so that those connections are already there by the time you have reached that point. You can set yourself deadlines and take them seriously, making sure you finish what you start on time as if it really was under contract. And you can always look ahead, finishing one project and then moving right on to the next one while you send the first out into the world.

- Even if you haven't snagged that first freelance gig, you can still practice reporting and delivering a piece on a deadline by starting a blog. Providing steady, quality content that way will not only help you build your audience but also a portfolio of work that can land you your dream job later.
- While you may not be a famous poet, you can still produce poems, submit to anthologies and contests and go to open mic nights to put yourself out there as you build up notoriety.

- Theatres may not be begging for your latest play yet, but you can still live the life of a playwright. Start by setting up your own readings and performances of your work with friends, all of which will help fine-tune your writing and get you to where you want to be.

- Even if you haven't achieved enlightenment from your meditative writing, you can still share your favorite lines from your morning pages. You never know what might inspire or strike a chord with someone else, making you a new fan or friend.

Give yourself goals. Pretend there are readers desperate for this next book that you will disappoint if it isn't out in time. Play the role of writing professional even though you're still the newest beginner. Focus on building a writing career of multiple works instead of obsessing over just this one.

It's not just a mental trick. It's a useful way to get yourself into the mindset you need to succeed in the writing life you want. At the same time, you're building up the habits, connections, and portfolio that will help get you there. And all that practice ensures you'll be better prepared to crush it when you do achieve that dream job.

But remember...

Don't get ahead of yourself

In an old Garfield book we had growing up, there's a week-long gag about him becoming a writer. In one comic, he says something like, "Lots of people say they want to write a book, but very few actually do something about it." The punchline is him, still having written nothing, sitting in front of the mirror in a smoking jacket saying, "Yes, this is how I will be photographed for my book jacket."

I think of this comic often because getting ahead of myself is a trap I fall into again and again. When I started writing my very first book,

I spent weeks researching the publishing industry, self-publishing, agents, submissions, author photos, and even marketing techniques when what I should have been doing was finishing my book. Because when I finished that book, and I was ready to put that research to use everything had changed so much, I had to start all over.

This industry shifts so fast, you're only wasting your time obsessing over a world that will be totally different by the time you're ready to publish and submit. The biggest favor you can do yourself and your future career is to finish writing the thing, and that means taking it all the way to the end and revising it until it's as good as you can make. Once you've finished whatever you're writing, you'll be both a better writer and more familiar with your work. Then you'll be able to make a more informed decision about what you want to do with it with the options available to you right now.

Finish it first, then worry about what comes next.

Fill your head with words by reading

Stephen King once said, "If you don't have time to read, you don't have the time (or the tools) to write. Simple as that."

To be a writer, you need to read. Read often. Read widely. Read what you know you'll love. Read what you think you'll hate. Fill your head with the rhythm of words and stories until it all can't help but come pouring back out on the page.

Reading makes you a better writer. Even when you're only reading for fun, you are learning how to craft a story, develop a character, and turn a phrase. Novels, plays, short stories, articles, non-fiction, graphic novels, audiobooks, they all level up your writing skill on a subconscious level while keeping you in the right mindset to write. And, yes, book snobs, graphic novels, eBooks and audiobooks are all "real books," and stories consumed that way are just as beneficial to your writing life as stories consumed any other way.

Read what you want to write.

If you want to write a particular genre, it just makes sense to read as much of that genre as you can. Not only because it helps you to understand the market and where your work might eventually fit but also to learn the tricks of the trade and the hallmarks of the genre. Moreover, reading the sort of thing you're writing can't help but give you more ideas for your work and keep you excited to finish it. You want to write romantic thrillers? YA paranormal? Personal essays? Then that's what you should read to see how it's done.

Read tangentially.

Maybe your book is a non-fiction analysis of the history of women in journalism. Alongside whatever you're reading for research for that book, for fun, you pick up a comic starring Superman's Lois Lane. While Lois Lane is a fictional character, elements of her story will run tangential to what you are working on, suggesting new angles to think about and avenues for research. While writing a story about flower fairies, you might read a gardening book or a mermaid novel while writing an article about Olympic swimmers. In all these cases, what you're reading isn't directly useful to what you are writing, but runs parallel enough to give you lots of food for thought you can bring back to your original idea.

Read what you like.

In the next section, we'll talk about how what you like to read and what you'll be good at writing go hand in hand. Similarly, there's nothing like reading a book you absolutely loved to invigorate you to go out there and create something of your own. After all, it's the writing we love that made most of us want to write in the first place.

Read outside your comfort zone.

Reading something I love puts me in a writing mood, but you know what really gets me fired up to write? When I read something I hate. Books that make me angry or are just so boring or annoying that I'm exasperated they even got published all send me dashing to my keyboard. Or, sometimes, I read something I think I will hate, and instead I love it, and it opens my eyes to a whole world I've never considered. That's pretty darn inspiring as well and can enrich your writing with new perspectives.

Read outside your gender, race, orientation, and nationality. Read books by and about people nothing like you. Try new formats, new genres, new authors, even if you're sure you won't like it. It's all broadening your writing worldview and making you a better writer.

Read to be a better writer.

Some writers won't read while they're writing because they are afraid they'll copy the other writer's style. While I suppose that's a risk if you are unusually impressionable, mimicking the style and voice of other authors is how you develop your own. Even if you end up borrowing their voice for a little while, you'll usually find that your own voice will come out stronger in the end.

As you build your writing life, make sure you build in time to read. It will help you increase your writing skills, understand the kinds of stories out there, and keep you in a storytelling frame of mind. And giving your brain new stimuli to think about can sometimes be just the thing to help get you unstuck in the whatever you're currently writing!

Let go of your Dumbo feathers

For years, I thought I could only write if I had the perfect circumstances. My favorite mood-setting music, my special writing spot in an inspirational setting and at least three hours of uninterrupted time. I rejected so many perfectly good moments when I could have been writing because I thought those ideal conditions were what I absolutely needed to write. It took me a long time to realize they were all just Dumbo feathers.

In the 1941 animated Disney movie, Dumbo the elephant is afraid to try to fly using his massive ears. The mouse, Timothy, promises him he'll be fine as long as he holds this magic feather. Dumbo clutches the feather with all his might, convinced it's the source of all his power and, hey, he can fly! But when Dumbo loses the feather at a critical moment, Timothy fesses up that the feather was a gimmick, an ordinary crow feather. The real power to fly was inside Dumbo all along. The token he depended on gone, Dumbo has to figure out how to trust himself to fly on his own.

This is one of the best metaphors there is for the creative life because so many of us convince ourselves that we need x or y to make the magic when the power was in us all along. I'm all in favor of silly gimmicks like writing hats or idyllic surroundings when you get stuck or to motivate on the hard writing days, but they can become a crutch. There's a big difference between knowing it's easier to write under certain conditions and becoming so dependent on them you fear you cannot write without them.

Like Dumbo, never forget that the power has been in you all along. You need nothing but you, your beautiful mind, and the words. That's it.

Take failure off the table

It was summer. My daughter was five years old and was just learning to go underwater. All-day long she'd done tentative little dips, dunking her face, sliding across the surface of the water.

Then she dropped her goggles. She lunged for them, but it was too late. Down down down, they sank to the very bottom of the deep end of the pool.

Over and over, she dipped under to get them, but she never even came close to where they were. With each dip, she got more frustrated. She was barely getting a foot under the water, how could she ever hope to get all the way down there to her goggles? She'd never even been down that deep before.

Finally, she snapped. She broke the surface after her latest attempt and screamed, "I quit!" With a roar of pure rage, she slapped at the water. "I QUIT!"

Before I could say anything comforting, she was back underwater, swimming, I assumed, for the ladder so she could get out and sulk. But, to my surprise, instead, she dove down, her legs kicking hard and fast. And before I could understand what I was seeing, she was all the way down there, down at the very bottom, grabbing her goggles and flying back up. She emerged from the water arm first, goggles held up triumphantly. I cheered.

"When I said I quit," she said matter-of-factly, "What I quit was failing. I quit quitting."

And then her goggles were back on her face, and she was diving under again, this time deeper and more confident than ever before.

If you want to do this writing thing, you need to quit quitting. You need to take failure entirely off the table. You need to commit to seeing this through. Because if you leave yourself that out, you can never kick as hard and fast towards your dreams as when you've promised yourself there is no other option.

Take it seriously

It may have been more taxing than you expected it to be but look what you accomplished! A stack of contracts lie before you, all signed and agreed upon. There were some ornery, stubborn fellows with long-held biases and weird hang-ups but they came around, and now everyone's on board. We're going to build you a writing life.

This is happening. You've got your mind wrapped around this writing thing. You're committed and determined to see it through, and that's a huge milestone.

Writing is an incredibly mental process, even before you're trying to weave a story with your words. As with any kind of creative work, you need to be in the right headspace to not only create but also to sustain it over the long haul. And while it can feel silly spending time wrapping your head around a concept instead of words down on the paper, it's an important step you'll revisit again and again throughout your writing career.

In this section, you made a mental commitment when you...

- Acknowledged that you are a writer, even with no fancy certification or publication glories to your credit.
- Gave yourself permission to write, even if that means writing badly because it's important to you.
- Prioritized writing in your life and saw where it ranked against your other priorities.
- Made the commitment to your writing and then made it real to you.
- Solidified why you write and what you want to get out of your writing.
- Converted your writing dream into a writing goal, something specific and concrete you can work towards.

- Told other people about your new writing journey to find your allies and writing tribe.
- Focused your attention on completing your writing goal without getting distracted by jealousy of other writers or getting ahead of yourself.
- Wrote for the job you want, not the one you have, by behaving professionally and taking the writing process seriously.
- Filled your head with stories and words by reading widely and often.
- Let go of your Dumbo feather and other gimmicks and remembered all you really need to write is yourself and the words.
- Quit quitting by taking failure off the table.

If there's a theme to everything we worked on so far, it's this: it's time to take writing seriously. This doesn't mean you can only write serious works. I write goofy slapstick fairy tales, but I still take the act of writing very seriously. You are setting goals and working towards them and taking the time to think about what it is you want. You made space in your head and committed to making this thing happen.

This doesn't mean you'll have no doubts or fears as you write because, unfortunately, those plague every writer at every level, but it does mean that now you are mentally contracted to building a writing life. And while there may still be unforeseen challenges along the way, it's this crucial first step that will let us move onto the next phase... writing!

BREAK GROUND

Start Writing

You can only stand around a table with architects and surveyors for so long... at some point, you have to start building. But look at that beautifully cleared space in front of you where there's nothing but dreams and potential. Bringing in excavators and jackhammers will make a huge mess. Things won't go as you've planned, they never do, and it will take a lot of dirty, sweaty WORK to make something happen there. It's so much easier to hold on to that beautiful fantasy than let it get sullied by pain and process.

If you've ever sat down to write and then found yourself staring at the blank page, paralyzed, you know this feeling well. The words in your head are so perfect and what you manage to get on the page can't compare. But while it's hard to imagine the finished house from a pile of boards and nails, you cannot achieve your writing dreams if you don't break ground.

It's time to actually start writing.

Write something.

Today.

Anything.

Yes, I am saying that it literally does not matter what you write. Writing is a muscle and the same basic skills apply to every form and genre. What's important at this point is writing anything at all to get over that initial fear of the blank page and comfortable with the act of getting words down.

Sit down at a keyboard or with a notebook and pen and see what comes out. It doesn't matter if it's a comic poem when you consider yourself a serious researcher or if it's a stream-of-consciousness rant about that loudmouth at the bank when you thought you'd be writing a novel. Writing the "wrong thing" often turns out to be the right thing. A poem may yield the perfect opening line for an article someday, a rant the motivation for the ultimate novel villain. No writing is ever a waste because you're always increasing your skills and fine-tuning your process.

Does it surprise you when your friend the war reporter writes the best birthday card messages? Or when it turns out your favorite romance author wrote that in-depth law article? Or that a playwright known for goofy fairy tale comedies is also an e-commerce specialist with a popular business blog? (Psst! That one's about me.)

It shouldn't. Writing is writing. The more you write, the better you get at writing, and that means any kind of writing. But so many new writers can't wrap their head around this idea.

Once you understand that every word counts, you can embrace the incredible freedom of knowing that you can write anything. Literally, whatever you want. Now is the time to play, to experiment, to discover what you can really do.

In this section, you'll start writing before you're ready and dive into the story of your heart. Try journaling and the meditative practice of Morning Pages. Learn how to find and nurture ideas from the world around you by combining writing what you like and know, mining your journal, and using prompts in your idea collection. Get your butt in the chair and show up to do the work of writing even when you don't feel like it and weigh the pros and cons of both editing as you write and writing fast. And, lastly, you'll decide what to write in from a simple notebook to sophisticated writing software.

And, most importantly, you'll start writing at last! So let's get to it!

"It's not as good as in my head!"

Does this sound familiar? You've got this fantastic scene in mind, the whole thing is just RIGHT THERE fully formed in your head, and all you need to do is write it down! You rush to your preferred writing implement, start to write and... things don't go quite how you pictured.

You expected your beautiful gazelle of an idea to leap directly from your imagination. Instead, you've got this newborn fawn lurching around the page. The distance between what's in your head and what's written is so far it feels like something must be wrong.

But there's nothing wrong. This is what it's like for all of us. There will be a significant difference between what you envision and what you write. And yet, if you haven't come to terms with this reality, this divide can make you doubt yourself and your abilities or even want to give up writing entirely.

Here's what you need to remember when you sit down to write your first draft of anything: this is not your last time through this. It's during the editing and revision process that you'll bring the words on the page closer to what you originally intended or maybe something even better. But to tinker and tweak what you write now into something more, you first need to write something. You cannot edit a blank page.

Let me tell you my trick for pushing through when it feels like all I'm doing is scrawling out a crayon drawing of the masterpiece in my head. I think of the Hollywood director assuring his fussy star, "Don't worry, babe, we'll fix it in post!" Have you ever seen how silly the raw footage of those big blockbusters look before they edit it together and add in all the special effects? As long as you've got something on film, you can always tweak it in the editing booth.

Write now and worry about fixing it later.

But write... what?

Maybe you sit down, and the words flow like magic. Sometimes it's like that, and it's a beautiful feeling. But often the blank page is paralyzing as if the mere act of thinking about writing dries up your creative well. You know you should write, should get words down and build up your writer's muscles, but what should you write?

Maybe there's THAT story, the one you feel you were born to tell, the one that's been begging you to tell it for half your life. Or maybe you've got hundreds of stories all beating down the door to get you to write them first. Whichever it is, go ahead and start on them. Yup, right now.

Start before you're ready

There's an expression in business that says successful people start before they are ready. You probably don't feel ready to work on THAT story now, but here's the thing: we're none of us ever truly ready to do something as scary as writing the story of our heart. There will always be a million excuses and fears and doubts telling you, "not yet." But too much preparation is itself just a form of procrastination.

Do it anyway. Rip off the bandage. Start it now.

Might you need to pause at some point and outline or research or figure out that back story? Sure! Go ahead and do that stuff too because that's also writing. But don't wait to start it.

If you are passionate about the story now, it's silly to wait, particularly because the more you write of your story, the more you'll have a better sense of what you need to do to finish it. Take that passion you have now, hold your nose, and dive in words first. You can figure out how to do everything else on the way down.

Follow your muse

A thing that surprises a lot of new writers is that authors don't always write books in the order they are read. Rarely does the author start with the first scene and write all the way to the end. It's also just as rare that a writer works on only one thing at a time. Juggling several projects at once is part of the writing life. I'm writing this book while I'm waiting for final edits on a short play and letting the first draft of another play cool.

Write the thing you want to write today. It may be five scenes after the last one you wrote. It may not be the same project as you worked on yesterday. No rule says you have to be consistent. So long as you finish the whole project, the reader will never know what order you wrote the scenes in or that you were working on several projects at the same time.

Don't fight your passion, work with it. If you are randomly excited about that one fight scene or to research the mating habits of sea slugs, do it! It's both easier and faster to work on the thing you want to be working on than to force what you think you should do instead.

Keep a journal

As a kid, I used to have one of those diaries with the little metal locks on it. I maybe wrote in it four times in my entire childhood, which is funny because I journal almost daily now. I use my journal for everything from jotting down funny things my kids said to in-depth analysis of how my business is going. I journal my way out of plot holes in my latest story, to figure out what do to next in my career, to rant about something bothering me in my personal life. Journaling is like a good talk with a friend... except that friend is yourself.

Without even trying that hard, you can find a dozen articles about the value of journaling in business, creative pursuits, and your personal life, but there's still this stigma against it. If you've got some hang up in your head that journaling isn't "real" writing, let me take a moment to assure you it is. In a way, journaling is the best kind of writing.

When you write in your journal, you know no one will ever see it but you. And knowing that no one will judge it or even read it at all takes the pressure off. This is why some of my absolute best writing has come from a random stream of consciousness I wrote in my journal. Journaling lets you write free of everything but you and your thoughts and that often unleashes ideas you'd never get when writing "on-stage."

Journaling is also a great way to get an idea out of your head and work it out. This can mean story problems like a sticky plot issue or experimenting with a character's voice, or it can mean trying to figure out more about your writing process itself, noting patterns in your work or problems that need your attention. It's also great to be able to refer back to your journal to remind yourself that you always doubt things at this point in a project or to discover how you worked your way through this problem the last time it happened. When I'm not sure what to work on, I start my writing session with a quick journal entry, and that almost always points me in the right direction.

So if you aren't already keeping a journal, now's a great time to start. Add to it whenever you feel stalled out on your main project just to keep your writing muscles fresh and your momentum up. If nothing else, it will give you a safe space to play with words without the pressure, and that will help you no matter what you later go on to write.

Writing as meditation: Morning Pages

Clear your mind. Set a timer for a small amount of time, such as 15-20 minutes. Then do nothing but write literally whatever comes to mind until the time is up, trying to get as many words down as possible. Some people call this a brain dump, stream of consciousness, or just free writing but it can also be a powerful form of meditation. And many believe it can be just as powerful as traditional meditative practices.

The idea of Morning Pages, i.e., this kind of free writing done first thing in the morning, is over 100 years old and involves a timed spontaneous writing burst as described above. While ideally done immediately after waking and by hand, you can do it at any time of day, via dictation (voice to text) or typed on a computer. Because you are getting the words down too fast to over-think or self-censor, you can achieve far more personal growth and self-discovery than through standard journaling. At the end of the session, read what you wrote aloud and underline the parts that speak to you the most.

Sound too crunchy for you? Try it anyway. A little timed writing can provide a calm and clarifying feeling to set the right tone for the rest of your day.

Night Notes or Evening Pages, done right before bed, are also a great way to unwind after a hectic day to put you in the best mindframe for a restful sleep. And just like with a journal, you'll often find that your best ideas and turns of phrase come from these personal pages.

Finding and nurturing ideas

If you don't already have an idea or two begging to be written, there are a few ways you can find writing ideas and nurture them into something worth writing about.

Ask, "What if?"

As a writer, get in the habit of asking, "What if?" and letting your imagination fill in the blanks. What if you were that streaker fleeing the SuperBowl grounds crew? What if flying cars really had been around in the 1950s? What if two presidential candidates who hate each other fell in love?

Fiction is reality with a twist. We all have random idle thoughts. The difference is that the writer mulls on them a little longer, letting them grow, seeing how they develop. Once you get in the habit of asking, "What if?" to the world around you, you'll find ideas everywhere.

Start an idea collection

Sometimes you see a good story idea in the morning newspaper. Occasionally it's inspired by a comment by a friend. Other times they pop into your head out of the nowhere.

Whenever you get an idea, no matter how random or incomplete, jot it down in your idea collection. This can be a digital or physical notebook or folder that you'll be able to add to as you find more ideas, the kind of thing you can build on over a writing lifetime.

While I'll sometimes jot an idea down on paper or clip something from a magazine or newspaper, I'll always move it to my digital notebook later. I prefer digital because then I always have it saved in the cloud so I can't lose it. I keep my idea collection in the free OneNote app because it has a lot of organizational features, supports handwriting, clipping and images and syncs to just about everything. Something like Google Docs or EverNote would work fine too. The format of your idea collection doesn't matter. What matters is collecting those grains of an idea when you get them because, no matter how certain you are that you'll remember them later, you almost certainly won't.

When you jot down the idea, do yourself a favor and take at least 5 minutes to write every random thought you have about that idea right now. This may be a few directions the story could take, lines or jokes you could imagine appearing in it, or just a few words about why you thought this idea was intriguing. If you find yourself thinking about this idea again, you can add to this page accordingly.

But taking the time to at least flesh out a bit of what drew you to this idea and what you would do with it does Future You a considerable favor. Otherwise, you end up someday staring at a piece of paper that just says, "Ghost cats. Robot?" wondering what in the world Past You might have meant by that.

Write what you know?

It's hard to think of a writing cliche more prevalent than, "Write what you know!" The problem is that it's not well understood and that confusion has lead many a would-be writer astray. Should you write what you know? Well, yes and no.

Write what you know

The roots of this expression come from the poor writer with no idea what to write, desperately scrounging around for a topic. Along comes a friend with sensible comfort: Write what you know! Make it easy on yourself and dig into the wealth of your own experiences, expertise, and memories to find your stories., no one else in the whole history of the world has lived your exact life, and that makes your perspective unique!

It's meant to be a helpful tip. After all, if you work as a barista, it makes sense that it'll be easier for you to write about a character that's also a barista than a nuclear physicist. You already have the first-hand experience to color your story, the insider knowledge of the world, and a familiar point of view to write from. Writing what you know is efficient, more comfortable, and means less research and legwork.

For this reason, it's an excellent idea to keep a list of things you know to add to your idea collection. Things you consider yourself an expert in, sure, but also your identity. The sum of your lived experiences and circumstances also tally up into what you know. This list provides another resource for inspiration and a place to dive for ideas whenever you want to write what you know.

The problem with write what you know

But like anything so oft-repeated, this phrase has a bad reputation. Without context, many a writer hears, "Write what you know" and thinks it means that's all they can write. With this reading, this advice feels like an edict from the writing gods on high and is incredibly limiting.

Of course, you can write well beyond what you know. You can imagine worlds that never existed, you can research those that did, you can understand someone nothing like you through sensitive study and the power of empathy. Could you imagine what a boring world it would be if we were all only limited to writing what we had experienced firsthand?

Write what you know.

Write what you don't.

Write it all.

There are no limits.

Mutate what you know

If you're still feeling tentative about writing what you don't know, let me share a trick I like to call "mutate what you know." It means taking the things you know and mutating them into something else.

I have never ridden a dragon. I have no idea what it feels like to be on one's back when it bursts into the sky or to give it an affectionate scratch after a good flight. I have never felt dragon fire bursting from my mount's mouth. Dragon riding is definitely not something that I know.

I have, however, ridden horses since I was small. I have felt a horse breathing under my legs. I know how to shift my weight when I feel it plant its legs before we launch into the air over a jump. I have also hung out with my friend's very chill lizard and watched its eyes half close when I tickled the soft scales under its chin. I have been too close to my parent's old barbecue when I finally got the darn thing to light, and I had to jump clear of the sudden fire.

There are all things I know and know well. I know how these moments smell, sound, and feel to the touch. A dozen real sensations I have experienced... and I bet you can already see how I could mutate each of them just a little to show you a scene of dragon-riding that felt real.

The things you know are tools at your disposal. They aren't your only tools, but they can still be handy in a surprising number of ways. The more you experience, the more you know, the more you have to draw from when you write. So don't just write what you know, but always work to increase the scope of what you know and grow your creative toolbox.

Write what you like

Grab a piece of paper or a blank document on your computer and make a list of things you enjoy. Your favorite books, video games, movies, and TV shows, your most cherished tropes, those topics that you can never seem to get enough of. From this list, make a second list of your very favorite elements of everything on the first list.

What themes, moments, or individual characters make your favorites work for you? You'll immediately notice patterns and things in common between your preferences. They can be broad like "anti-heroes," "love triangles," or "comic action sequences," or something much more niche like "sassy old lady mechanics." My mom once told me she loves "any film where Shia LaBeouf is stressed" and, while I'm pretty sure that's not an officially recognized genre, I'll bet you know exactly what she means.

Keep this list safe in your idea collection. Whenever you think of something else to add to it, do so, and grow it as you go. Because what you've created here is not just a list of your favorite things to watch, play and read, it's also a list of the things you'll want to write. The more you enjoy something, the easier and more enjoyable it will be for you to write it. Therefore your favorite things to consume are the same things you'll want to go to when you're writing.

But it doesn't mean that this list is all you can write or that it should limit you. Absolutely not! But if you find yourself stuck for something to write, pull this list out and try combining some of your favorite things to see what comes out. (This trick also works great when you're stuck in a story!) It's much easier to write when the story is made up of everything you love anyway.

Mine Your Journal

A few sections ago, we talked about some reasons keeping a journal is a writer's secret weapon, but there's one more benefit we didn't touch on. Your journal can be an absolute wealth of inspiration and writing ideas! Private entries polish up into memoir material or personal essays. Family memories or work anecdotes are ripe for fictionalization in short stories and novels. Those topics you revisit again and again in your journal are an excellent starting point for articles and freelance pieces.

Because you don't journal intending to share it, you're able to be more raw and authentic. This can mean better writing because there's no artifice or attempt to impress. Less self-conscious writing means you make connections or unearth ideas without even realizing it. When you revisit this writing later with a little emotional distance, you'll find plenty you've still got more to write about.

Use Prompts

There are a ton of books and websites out there that offer prompts for writers, and they are a great thing to turn to when you are stuck for what to write about. Search "writing prompts" or "random prompt generator," and you'll see that there are hundreds of options. Some give you a question or statement to start with while others offer you a first sentence, a single word, or even an image for you to use for inspiration.

Once you have a prompt, give yourself a set amount of time and see what comes out! Going into a writing session with no pre-set idea and giving your topic over to the whim of the random prompt generator is an easy way to set your creativity free and uncover insights you'd never have thought of otherwise. It can often take your imagination in unexpected directions with amazing results!

Mix 'n Match

You have your journal. You have your list of favorite things and things you know. You have your idea collection. And you have prompts to turn to when all else fails. While ideas can come from any of those sources alone, you can also use them in combination to make connections and mash-ups that spark your imagination. When you take the time to collect and organize your ideas, unconnected bits of inspiration sometimes link up in unexpected ways.

For example, I add a local newspaper story about a woman who fought off a bear with a wrench to my idea collection. Then I link that to "sassy old lady mechanics" that I have on my list of favorite things. I find the final part in my journal, a memory of my grandma fighting off a bat with a hammer, and that gives me the emotional piece I was missing to turn this into a proper story.

These were three random ideas I'd collected that suddenly linked together. But I wouldn't have been able to do it if I hadn't been both collecting and keeping my eye out for story ideas all along. Doing the work to seek stimuli and then writing those bits of ideas down as you go makes it much easier to connect those pieces whenever you're stuck for something to write.

Butt in chair

Another bit of writing advice you'll see a lot is, "Butt in chair!" But what the heck does that mean? I can do a heck of a lot of things with my butt in a chair that have nothing whatsoever to do with writing! I also do a fair amount of writing without my butt in any kind of chair at all between dictation and my standing desk.

The expression Butt in Chair means you have to show up. Spend the time you set aside for writing actually writing and not checking Facebook or taking the perfect #amwriting selfie. Practice butt in chair habitually if you want to improve and make progress.

If this is a struggle, there are a lot of apps and browser extensions available to help you focus. Distraction blockers like StayFocused or Freedom let you block sites you know are distracting, or the whole dang internet, so you have no choice but to write. Other apps, like Forest, reward you for resisting the urge to look at your phone or browser. But low tech options, like a simple egg timer, writing in a paper notebook or just switching off the wifi/data on your device, work too.

Elsewhere in this book, I talk about the myth that writers must write every day and, spoiler alert, I don't believe in it. I write a TON and I sure as heck don't write every day. I think it's much more important to write regularly than to worry about writing every single day.

That said, last summer, I took on a daily writing streak challenge for a few months because I was in a funk and needed something to kick me back into gear. And, while daily for me meant I stayed up late and wrote on both sides of midnight so I only had to write every other day, I still discovered something amazing. I got a whole lot written that summer.

Turns out, if you write more often... you get more writing done! Mind-blowing, I know, but it turns out that more time writing apparently equals more words. I mean, who knew, right?

But while this revelation may seem painfully obvious, it's worth mentioning because sometimes we all fall into the trap of thinking magic elves will work on our story when we're away from it. Regular writing, even if it's only a bit at a time, will mean steady progress, and that moves you ever closer to your writing goals. But to do that you've got to keep showing up, ready to write, with your butt in chair.

Butt in chair is about committing to whatever writing regularly means to you. It's about setting a schedule, sticking to it and making sure you spend all of that allotted time actually writing. And when you do that, you'll see an immediate change in your writing skills and process.

Not to mention, get a heck of a lot more writing done!

It starts somehow

Sometimes you sit down, butt in chair, just like you're supposed it and... you've got nothing. Or you've got something, but it's stuck in your head, and you can't seem to get any of the words down the page. And all the while, the blank page just sits there still so empty, mocking you.

Even after years of writing and hundreds of projects started and finished, I still get that same gulping fear when I open a blank page for the first time and start something new, and I want to share a silly little trick I've developed to help with this. If I don't have a beginning ready to go, I simply start typing the words, "It starts somehow."

If I generally know what I want from the beginning, I add a few notes about it after that sentence. So the document would start with a little paragraph like this:

> *It starts somehow. Ideally, in some kind of brilliant way that shows the darkness she'll embrace at the end but subtly, so it's mostly lighthearted. Should also establish the circus. The central image could be the tent going up to mirror the end when it falls?*

And then I jump down a line or two and start writing whatever part I feel like I've got a handle on and go from there.

While that first paragraph won't appear in the final version of whatever I'm writing, it accomplishes two things that make it easier to continue. The first is that it fills up some of the page so there's already something there and it's less intimidating when I start to write in earnest. And secondly, though I'm talking to myself, I'm still writing and thinking about what I'm about to write which gets my head in the right space to do the job for real.

The most important thing to remember about beginnings of any kind is that they don't matter as much as it feels like they do and they almost always change. You can always rewrite or revise whatever you write now later. So don't sweat coming up with the perfect beginning. Just start, somehow, and move forward from there.

The Editing Question

Some writers write slowly, taking the time to pick the perfect word and clean up sentences as they go. Others just dump words on the page as fast as they can and don't edit any of it until they reach the end of the draft. Which way is right?

My personal style is to write quick and dirty first drafts and not even think about editing until the next pass through. I'll only stop to fix something if it's such a mess I don't think I'll remember what I was saying when I look at it later. Otherwise, I keep writing my way forward without ever looking back until the end. I end up changing so much during the revision process, stopping to do any editing while writing the first draft feels like pausing the dryer mid-cycle to fold the clothes only to throw them right back in there to get jumbled up again.

But that's just me. Because this is so tied to your personal preference and writing process, there's no way for me to tell you which is right for you. The one thing I will say is that if you find you spend a lot of time tweaking what you're writing and not a lot of time making forward progress or finishing things, you may need to lock your inner editor away for a while until you finish the draft because she's slowing your progress. On the flip side, if you're writing so fast that your drafts are incoherent and basically useless to you, then it might be worth slowing down and doing a little more clean up as you go.

Remember: this is not your last time through this. There will be time to tinker and get it right, but you've got to actually write the thing first. Finishing is more important than fine-tuning.

When should I hire an editor?

While I don't want to get ahead of ourselves, let's jump into the future for a minute to answer one of the most frequently asked writer questions of all time: When should you hire an editor to go over your writing? The answer is: Once you have fully completed the work, revised it several times yourself, and know it is the absolute best that you can make it on your own.

Not immediately after you finish your draft. Not when you're "basically almost finished." Not when you know it still needs a lot of work but don't feel like doing it. When you've done the work to polish and improve your manuscript and know there is nothing else you can do it to make it better on your own, it's time to bring in an editor. That goes for content editing, which is the big picture structural revision for plot, characters, pacing, etc. as well as copy-editing, the very last stage before publication where you clean up spelling, grammar, and punctuation.

For one, editing is not cheap. You'll only be wasting your money having someone edit an early draft that will fundamentally change during the revision process. And, more importantly, an editor can only work with what you give them, and if what you give them isn't complete or even your best work, that's what you'll get back. Bringing an editor onto your project too soon can discourage or distort your project into something other than what you intended and be a big waste of time. Time that's better spent leveling up your writing craft and skills as you work to improve what you wrote before you bring in the pros.

Think of it this way: You're getting work done in your backyard, construction trucks in and out every day, churning up the lawn. Do you bring in a landscaper to plant a beautiful row of flowers in the path those trucks pulverize every day or do you wait until the whole project is done, the ground smoothed, and grass reseeded, and then add that finishing touch? I think you know the answer.

Writing Speed

How fast do you write? Do you know your actual your words per minute? It's worth figuring out for setting deadlines and planning projects. It's particularly handy for when you see an opportunity you want to submit to because you can figure out whether you can realistically finish something on time for it or not.

If you're only writing for yourself, then your writing speed doesn't matter. You can take your time and revel in the words and work at whatever pace is the most comfortable. But if you've got your eyes set on publication, then you'll often have deadlines and other external pressures to factor in so you'll have to think about your writing speed.

Whether or not you edit as you write will have a significant effect on your words per minute, but that's not all there is to it. Some of us are Stephen King, steadily churning out six pages a day without fail, and others are George R. R. Martin, carefully crafting a single chapter for months on end. Something more complicated, like a research project, will take longer than something you're making up on the spot. Other factors that can effect your writing speed are how consistent your writing schedule is, whether you type, handwrite or use dictation, and also your personal health both physical and mental.

Write fast or write slow. Neither is wrong nor right, and your personal preferences rule which one you choose. If one speed works for you, that's the one you should use. But if you're brand new to this writing thing or have been struggling to ever finish a writing project, I highly recommend trying to gradually increase your writing speed over time.

Advantages to Increasing Your Writing Speed

I type pretty fast. Whenever people ask me about my typing speed, I always credit the fact that terrifying nuns drilled the home row style of typing into me in Catholic elementary school and, to this day, I still type like those intimidating ladies are watching over my shoulder.

One time I was explaining this origin story to another writer who scoffed. "I can type fast," they said, "but I can't write fast because I have to think about what I'm going to write first!" And they were so smug about this, I didn't know what they wanted to hear in response. Because, obviously, I also have to think of what to write before I put it down on paper. No one is beaming me ideas direct from Neptune or anything!

But when you get in the habit of writing faster, your thinking speeds up accordingly. We often can't tell the difference between thinking and overthinking when we're in the thick of a writing session, and the latter only slows us down and wastes our precious writing time. When you increase your speed, you don't have time for thinking about anything that isn't essential for getting words down.

There are some excellent reasons I recommend gradually increasing the speed you write, especially when writing your first draft.

Outrun your fears.

When you write slowly, it's too easy to question every word choice, your own abilities and get so bogged down in every tiny detail that you doubt the whole thing. But when you fly through the words, your brain has to move so fast it forgets to be afraid or second guess. You create a direct conduit between the words and the page, and that can make a world of difference in achieving your writing goals. When you stop over-thinking every word, you bypass your inner editor creating an unbroken line between your imagination and fingers. And that auto-pilot, my friend, where ideas feel like they are flying out of nowhere, is as close to a magical feeling as you can get with writing.

Keeps the goal moving steadily closer.

One of the hardest things about writing a whole book is the sheer scope of the project and the absolute mountain of words you have to write. But when you move through your draft quickly, the whole project is less intimidating because you can see the ending getting closer and closer with every writing session. That progress can be essential to keeping you motivated through to the end.

Reminds you that words are cheap.

On multiple occasions, I have written 2,000 words in a single 15-minute sprint. Now imagine it's time to edit, and it turns out I have to cut those 2,000 words. Who do you think that cut hurts more for? Me, who only lost 15 minutes of work, or the person who spent most of a week to write that much? When you write a lot, particularly when you write fast, you're not as precious about what you wrote, and that makes you a better writer because you're more willing to cut or change those words as needed later.

Quantity begets quality.

The more often you write, the better you get. Just as your muscles get stronger the more you work out, every word you get down helps you to hone your writing craft and improve.

Writing fast = writing more.

What if you could get more writing done in every writing session? The more you write each day, the closer you get to achieving your writing dreams. And that means...

Get more done in less time.

If you could finish your daily writing in half an hour instead of three and then play video games all night, why wouldn't you? I write fast because I don't have a lot of time, but I have a lot of ideas and things I want to have written in my lifetime so I gotta hustle if I'm going to get them all done.

Race yourself or others for motivation.

I'm a spreadsheet junkie, and I use the data I keep about my writing to motivate me. I'm always pushing myself to beat my previous records like my highest word count days or longest writing streak. If you are a competitive sort, it's fun to race other writers or even your own past times in sprints or other short writing bursts. When you focus on getting as much done as you can in the time you have, you can discover you are capable of things you never thought possible.

When I have something like a critical email, I go through it nice and slow, word by word, because I only have one chance to get it right. But almost every other time I'm writing it's something I'll have plenty of time to revise and clean up later. And it makes little sense to me to slow down to tinker with words only I'll cut or change later. Plus I'm a bit impatient and a lot pressed for time, so I'd always rather whip through the draft as fast as possible to move onto the next stage.

If you want to try increasing your speed, word sprints are a great way to start. Once you know how much you write in a timed writing burst, you can begin to gradually increase that. Dictation is also great for improving your words per minute because most of us talk a lot faster than we can type. Planning what you will write ahead of time can also increase how quickly you can write since you won't have to slow down to think of what's next. If you think it's the mechanics themselves tripping you up, do some typing practice and learn touch typing to eliminate the hunting and pecking and up your accuracy. Don't be surprised if your joints and muscles may rebel at first until they get used to your new writing pace.

Just like building up a writing habit, increasing your writing speed also becomes second nature with time. I struggled for years to get anywhere near 50,000 words done in a single month, I now regularly write that in a fraction of that time. Of course, you shouldn't try to increase your speed at the expense of what works for you and your writing process but, if you are looking to get more out of every writing session, it's well worth speeding up a bit to see what it does for you.

Where to put the words

It's one thing to say, "Start writing!" but you may wonder, ok, but like... how? Literally, where should I be putting the words? What should I be writing in?

Technology has provided us an absolute glut of choices for ways to write from mobile apps for writing on the go to desktop software with advanced organizational features. As for what is the best option for you, it all comes down which one is the easiest and most comfortable. It doesn't matter if everyone swears by this fancy software if you get a headache just trying to figure out all its features. There are no wrong answer here, so don't stress too much about where you are putting the words and just get them any way you can.

That said, let's look at the pros and cons of a few of the most popular options, so you know what's out there.

Write on whatever's handy

You know where I write my first drafts? On whatever's handy. Emails to myself, memos on my phone, notes handwritten on random scraps of paper. Chapters aren't just spread out between multiple files, every scene was likely written differently. (I'm editing this very book, and the font in this part differed from the last because I wrote them in different programs.)

I am not even remotely picky about how I write my first drafts. That's because, for the first draft, what matters most is getting the words down any way I can, not how or where I wrote them. My only rule is that I name the files something useful so I can find them again and date each section so I can put them in order later but, other than that, it's a writing free for all!

When it comes time to edit, I collect all those random bits and pieces together in an organized way to assemble my first draft. I don't mind taking the time to do this because I would much rather slow down and do a little organization before revising than slow myself down during the actual writing by worrying about what I'm writing in.

The beauty of words, particularly when it's digital text, is that, once written, it's easy to transfer words from one program or medium to another. When the ideas are flowing, and you are ready to write, it doesn't matter where you do that writing. You can always move those words around later once you've got them down.

Writing by hand

There's something about taking a favorite pen and a pretty notebook and just letting the words pour out. It's an almost magical process where ideas can flow directly through your hand through the satisfying physical sensation of ink on paper. Or so I've been told since my joints are so bad I can't handwrite for more than a few minutes before my fingers cramp up in pain.

Writing by hand is not for everyone. But if it's what works for you, don't let our gizmo-loving world discourage you from going low tech.

Advantages of writing by hand

Feels different from typing. There is something to that physical sensation of scratching words out on the paper. Even if it's not an everyday solution, writing by hand can be a great way to free up ideas when you're stuck or a way to change things up once in a while.

Very portable. It's easy to leave a small notebook in your car or daily bag and take it on the go.

Advantages of going low tech. A paper notebook isn't just light, it also doesn't need batteries, a plug and outlet, have delicate ports or a breakable screen. This allows for more creative writing spots where you might not want to risk your pricey tech like alongside a beautiful mountain stream or on the beach.

Fewer distractions. There's no way to access the internet from a piece of paper, no emails or notifications to pull your attention and no red squiggly lines to tell you when you spelled a word wrong. All of that makes it easier for you to just write without all the noise.

Easier to let go of your first draft. One of the hardest things for new writers to do when revising is letting go of their first draft. If the words you already wrote are right there in the document, why do the work of finding a better way to tell the story? But when you handwrite, you'll end up rewriting everything anyway with each draft which makes it easier to cut and change things while you're at it.

Disadvantages of writing by hand

You can't publish something handwritten. While handwriting is great for journaling and other personal writing, you'll have to type it in eventually if you have commercial plans because the publishing industry works with digital files. This adds an extra step to just about every part of the writing process from revision to publication.

There's no backup. If you lose your notebook or spill your coffee on it, that's it! The words are gone.

No cloud access. Because you're writing in a physical notebook, there's always the trap of forgetting it or feeling like you can't write unless you have it.

Hard to translate or share what you wrote. To the eternal dismay of my first-grade teacher who tried to scare good penmanship into me, I have the worst handwriting in the entire world. Sometimes I can't even read my writing and forget about giving something I wrote by hand to a beta reader or typist who'd never be able to interpret it. Turns out, sometimes those squiggly red spelling lines are a good thing!

Can be hard on the hands. If you're not used to writing by hand, you'll also learn pretty quickly that the muscles in your hand will need time to work up to regular writing so don't be surprised if you joints rebel like it's essay test day in high school.

Writing Software

What kind of computer program should you write in? You really only need a basic text box or bare-bones word processor. But if you want something with more features, we're in a golden age for writing software, and there are hundreds of choices out there. It's, frankly, overwhelming, and a little intimidating to pick one. But, as with anything, making a choice should be about finding the option that you find the most comfortable and works best with your needs.

That said, the right writing software can be a tremendous time-saver and organizational lifesaver, so don't be afraid to take advantage of free trials when available and test things out. You can always write your first draft one way and then move to fancy software later when you've progressed onto other phases like revision and publication. As you may have guessed from my chaotic method of writing first drafts in whatever's handy, I'm a big believer in not even bothering to put my words into writing software until the later drafts. (For plays, this means my first drafts are not in script format at all until the revision process.)

I recommend giving any writing program a thorough trial before you commit to using it for your big project. Get good and comfortable with it, kick the tires, see what that baby can do. You don't want the learning curve, or other tech hang-ups, slowing you down when you're just trying to get the story down.

Because there are so many options out there with more coming out every day, I can't even attempt to review them all. Instead, here's a list of things you'll want to consider when choosing writing software.

Your ideal writing program should...

- Automatically save your work and let you restore previous versions, so you never lose your work.
- Have a way to back up your work to the cloud or another machine. If you're only saving to your local device, you'll lose all your writing if your computer dies.
- Import your writing to common formats like .doc, .rtf, or .pdf, especially if you plan on sharing or publishing your work later.

Other features that aren't essential but I would highly recommend...

- Basic spelling and grammar check to catch the most glaring errors.
- Calculate your word count or provide other ways to track your progress.
- Mobile or cloud-based writing option for writing on the go.
- Have some kind of organizational system for not only writing files but also research, brainstorming, outlining, etc.
- Be able to handle large text documents, particularly if you plan to write a whole book.

Keep in mind that you may need to use a second program or your own personal tricks to make your favorite choice work as described above. For example, many professional writers use Microsoft Word even though Word notoriously crashes while handling novel-length text files. But if that's the program you're most comfortable in, you can to find workarounds to its quirks like chopping the book into multiple files or allocating more RAM to the program to get it to function to suit your needs.

Similarly, though the popular writing software Scrivener doesn't have any native cloud back-up option, you can create one by using Dropbox or Google Drive file sync. Just because your preferred program doesn't do everything you want doesn't mean you can't make it work. But if you have to construct an elaborate network of hacks and tricks to get a program to run how you need it to, it might be well worth simplifying your life and trying something else that has all those features built-in.

Another consideration is cost. The new trend with writing software is a monthly fee. While it may be worth it to pay for something that works exactly the way you want it to, there are plenty of fantastic free options (Google Drive, OneNote, yWriter) or programs you can purchase for a one time fee and use forever (Scrivener). The monthly payment is a psychological trick because you think, "Oh, only $29. That's not much!" forgetting that means that amount every month for the rest of your writing life. It can really add up! Make sure you've thought the costs through before falling in love with a program and committing the time to set up your writing there.

For first drafts, there are some gimmicky options like Write or Die or Written Kitten that encourage you to get the words down as fast as you can but then let you export the words elsewhere once you're finished.

While I write first drafts in whatever's handy, I do use a variety of other programs after that. Exactly what writing program I use depends on what I'm writing.

For journaling, my idea collection and what I think of as "backstage writing" (character studies, outlining, brainstorming, etc.) I use Microsoft's OneNote app because it is free, works on every platform including mobile, has cloud saving, a myriad of organization tools and even lets you handwrite with a stylus on a phone or tablet. OneNote enables you to create digital notebooks which you can then divide into sections and pages. It's also got a ton of extra features other programs don't like To-Do lists, tagging, and drawing but doesn't display word count which drives me bonkers.

For mostly all writing I plan to publish (which includes scripts, novels and non-fiction like this), I use Scrivener. I'll be the first to admit that the learning curve for Scrivener is steep, but tutorials are your friend. It has a lot of powerful organizational tools that have become essential to my writing process, and I really miss them if I try to write in something else. It does the script formatting I need as a playwright, and it exports to just about everything when it's time to publish. Scrivener also makes it very easy to import all the random bits of my first draft that I wrote here and there in other programs into one document. Of the non-free writing programs, Scrivener is my favorite because of their very generous free trial and the fact that they only charge a one-time fee (off which NaNoWriMo participants and winners get significant discounts) when so many of their competitors charge a lifetime monthly.

For everything else, I use Google Docs. If you like Microsoft Word, Docs is almost identical. The difference is that Docs is free, makes it easy to search and organize files, and, though you can use it offline, it's mostly on the cloud, so everything is always backed up. You can also access it from almost any device. If you have a Gmail address or an account with Google or YouTube, you already have a Docs account and can use those logins to access it.

If you're just getting started and not attached to any particular writing program yet, try some of the options out there and see what you like. As my list above shows, even I haven't committed to any one program in particular but instead use a combination to achieve what I need. As long as whatever you choose has a way to easily save and import your words, you can always take them with you to another program later. It's the words themselves that matter, after all, not what you write them in!

What I wish I'd known

I'm not sure one can ever truly finish learning the craft of writing and, as with anything, your mileage may vary with just about any tip or supposed truism. That said, it doesn't seem right to leave this section without at least giving you a quick list of a few more things I wish I'd known before I started writing in earnest. While you'll have to learn some of this stuff on your own for it to sink in, I hope at least some of this advice will save you time and frustration if you know it up front.

- **Start before you're ready.**
- You can edit even the worst writing. **You cannot edit a blank page.** Having anything written is always better than nothing.
- **What you write on the paper will seldom be as good as it is in your head.**
- **First drafts are almost always an unmitigated disaster.** My favorite quote about first drafts is Shannon Hale saying, "I'm writing a first draft and reminding myself that I'm simply shoveling sand into a box so that later I can build castles."
- **You don't need to be inspired to write well or even at all.** In fact, getting used to writing when you're not in the mood is the key to making real writing progress.
- The process is different every time for every project. **What worked last time might not work this time** so you may need different tricks to make it through.

- **Almost every time you're stuck, it's because you don't have enough information yet.** Figure out what you don't know, and you'll find the way through.
- Writing is mostly mental, but it's also physical. **It's much easier to write when you're taking care of yourself.** Eat right, get enough sleep, stay hydrated, take the medicines you need to function and, most of all, remember to take breaks and leave time for fun.
- **Sometimes the best thing for your writing is to take a day off from it.** Play a game, take a walk or the night off, and you'll come back at it fresh the next day. Mindless activities, such as doing some housework (laundry! dishes!), are also great ways to unravel a stuck plot.
- **The solution to almost every writing problem is more writing.** When in doubt, throw more words at it!
- **Everyone's writing process is different.** What works for someone else may not work for you, and that's fine.
- **Comparing yourself, your writing, or your career to others is seldom a good idea.**
- **There is no One True Path for writing/publishing/etc.,** and anyone who tells you otherwise is selling something.
- **Finish it first, then worry about what comes next.**
- It's a small industry with a long memory. Be nice. Be professional. **Don't be a jerk.** Make friends that can support and help you, not enemies that can sink your chances.
- No matter how together it looks from the outside, trust me, **nobody else has any clue what they are doing either.** Once you realize that, it's strangely comforting.

Ready? Set? Write!

You've done it! You've started writing. You've broken ground on your new writing life. While it may be messy, sometimes it's necessary to get a bit of dirt on our hands to do great things.

In this section, you broke ground on your writing life when you...

- Started writing!
- Experimented with journaling and using it to both document and understand your life
- Started on that big idea, even if you weren't ready.
- Realized that sometimes you need to write what you want to write that day, even if it means jumping around and writing the story out of order or working on multiple projects at the same time.
- Found and nurtured ideas by building up your idea collection and combining inspiration from different sources.
- Planted your butt firmly in the chair to build up a writing habit.
- Started somehow, knowing you can always go back and change it later.
- Weighed the pros and cons of editing as you write and writing fast.
- Decided what to write in from paper notebooks to fancy writing software.

So you're writing now, and it's wild and exciting and probably a bit all over the place, but that is fine! At this point, we're just playing around in the dirt, trying to get our footing. Experiment, create, and enjoy the freedom of playing with words.

Next, we start to build up some structure.

BUILD A SOLID FOUNDATION

Establish a Writing Habit

Once you've gotten past the initial hurdle of breaking ground on your shiny new writing life, it's time to build yourself a solid foundation. That means making writing a regular habit, a sturdy, reliable thing you can always depend on to hold everything else up. It's about building on those occasional writing sessions, developing some discipline, and making writing a consistent part of your life.

There's excitement to starting anything new, and that can fuel you for a long time. But what about when the novelty wears off and what was fun feels like work? When the going gets tough, what will keep you writing?

A good foundation doesn't just hold the whole house up. It's customized to fit the structure above it, insulated to keep out cold and moisture and reinforced to keep the house steady if the earth moves around it. In the same way, you'll tailor your writing habit to fit your individual needs. The best writing habit is a shield against the chill of fears and doubts but still sturdy enough that it can survive any shake-ups life has planned.

A foundation is a permanent thing. If you're really going to do this, make writing a consistent part of your life, finish that big project, or build your writing career, you need to get settled in for the long haul. That means taking writing from being a thing you do once in a while to a routine that's solid as a slab of poured concrete.

In this section, you'll build up a writing habit by writing daily or at least regularly, removing obstacles to make it easier on yourself to write and learn tricks for self-motivation. Then you'll delve into how to set better goals, specific, realistic, and flexible goals where you break your big dreams down into smaller steps you can take every day. Then you'll ensure you're backing your writing up often, so you don't lose your hard work in an emergency, and then look into ways to keep your writing work safe and private online.

Build a writing habit

Why build a writing habit? What's the advantage of writing regularly rather than just when you feel like it? There are several big reasons.

Build up your writing muscles

The runner jogs every day to prepare for the big marathon, and daily training and exercise does the same thing for the writer. As with any regular activity, it may be a struggle to keep up at first, but, in time, you'll be stronger and able to do more than you thought possible.

Writing becomes second nature.

You don't think about brushing your teeth every day; you do it automatically as a part of your routine. It feels weird when you forget to do it, and it'd have to be something drastic that would make you skip it.

When you write regularly, writing becomes like that. It becomes such a natural part of your life that going too long without it feels wrong. Like muscle memory, you keep getting the words down because it's what you always do.

If you're just starting out, you often need to work extra hard to motivate yourself to keep writing with any consistency but, once you establish your writing habit, it's a lot easier to sit down to write each time because it becomes second nature. A writing habit is important because, with one, when the going gets tough, you're more likely to keep going than quit because writing has become something comforting and familiar in your life. The habit itself becomes what sustains your writing and compels your forward progress.

Repetition breeds confidence.

Remember the first time you drove a car by yourself? It was exhilarating and somewhat terrifying that someone let you be in charge of such a massive machine. But now, you drive so often that you zone out half the time you're behind the wheel. You barely think about it.

Right now, writing is still a new and somewhat scary thing because of the novelty of it. But it's incredible the change that happens when you write regularly for a while. It makes writing go from feeling like this epic process to, ho-hum, that thing I do every day.

Not that writing gets boring (because it doesn't, no matter how long you've been at it) but you become more confident in your abilities, your process, and your voice. It's impossible not to improve at just about anything with consistent practice and writing is no exception. It also takes the pressure off when it no longer feels like a special, once in a while process.

All that writing adds up.

Turns out, if you keep writing consistently, it really adds up! The beauty of regular writing, even if it's only a little each day, is that the finished pages collect quickly. It may seem like a somewhat obvious point that writing more often equals more writing overall and faster progress toward your writing goals, but it's still a surprising and very satisfying thing to witness in practice.

Think about it. If you were writing at least 500 words every day, you could finish an entire 100,000-word novel in under 200 days. Remember the tortoise and the hare? Slow but steady wins the race.

Easier to pick up where you left off

Have you ever come back to something you were working on after a break and wasted half your writing time rereading everything that came before trying to remember where the heck you left off? One of the best things about regular writing is that it reduces the time spent getting caught up and increases the time spent writing. Because you're checking in with your work in progress more often, it's fresh in your head so you can just sit down and get right down to it from where stopped yesterday.

The consistency also makes it easier to write overall. Because you're looking at your piece so frequently, you're more likely to be thinking about it between work sessions. This helps you see connections between ideas, come up with that perfect phrasing or work through plot issues because you're so closely living in the world of your story. It all makes for better first drafts and faster revision because you have the benefit of that continued closeness with your project.

Get used to writing when you're not inspired.

As E. B. White once said, "A writer who waits for ideal conditions under which to work will die without putting a word on paper." When I was first toying with being a writer, I had this very romanticized notion of what I needed to write. I needed to have perfect silence, a big chunk of time when I was sure not to be interrupted, and plenty of inspiration. As you can imagine, such moments were rare indeed. I only ended up writing a few times a year.

Now I write in whatever circumstances present themselves. Dictating on my phone while making dinner. Typing on my tablet while the baby naps on my lap. Sitting on the couch with my laptop while my six-year-old sings Let It Go at the top of her lungs into a wireless karaoke microphone with the echo effect turned up WAY too high. Whatever works to get the words down. Writing while inspired, alone or with silence are all things I'd prefer... but I realized a long time again I don't really need any of them to write and that freed up a lot of writing time I previously wouldn't have considered. And nothing helps you to get over being precious about your writing process like making it a part of your routine alongside all the other chaos.

The fact is, if we all only wrote when inspired or had ideal circumstances, nothing would ever get written. It's when you use your routine and get into the habit of writing when you don't feel like it that you start to make real progress on your big projects. And the good news is that the writing you churn out under less than ideal conditions because of habit and the writing you lovingly craft while in a magic trance of inspiration come out the same quality when you look at them later.

Write every day?

There is a lot of writing advice that says "Real Writers write every day" and this is gate-keeping nonsense. For that matter, you can go ahead and ignore anyone that is trying to define who the "Real" Writers are because there is no such thing. Writers are people that write, and that is all there is to it. Period.

But the write every day thing persists because it works well for many people. If you're aiming for consistency, it's hard to get more consistent than daily. People who write daily set a small goal, something like 250-500 words, 15-30 minutes or even a single page or two of writing, something they know they can accomplish in a short amount of time even on the most hectic day.

That said, writing daily may not work for you, and that's fine too. One of the biggest problems with aiming for daily writing is that if you miss a day or two, it can be incredibly discouraging. Because this myth of writers needing to write every day persists, you can also get frustrated or down on yourself when you find you can't sustain a daily habit.

Me, I write nothing even remotely close to every day. My life is too erratic to adhere to any consistent writing routine, so I write when I get the chance without sweating if it's daily or not. Even if you have a predictable schedule, it's not unreasonable to want a day off from writing to take a break, regroup, do administrative work for your writing career (So. Many. Emails!) or other things either tangential to your writing life or essential to your self-preservation.

Which is why it's much better to aim for writing regularly than daily. You want enough consistency that you're never going so long between writing sessions that you struggle to get back into it but on a schedule that works for you. The key is to integrate writing into your life in a way that you can realistically keep up with.

If you like to write daily, go for it! But if you can't, don't worry about it. Consistency and regularity are more important than daily in the long term.

Eliminate obstacles and excuses

With any new habit, there's always a certain amount of resistance to adding something to your established routine, so the easier you make it on yourself to write, the more likely you will. The status quo is comfortable and the path of least resistance while writing is still something new and unfamiliar. As soon as you give yourself that out of, "Well, I could write right now but..." your brain will take that excuse. One of the best things you can do for your writing habit is to examine the excuses you give yourself for not writing and see how you can render them moot.

For example, if you're always lamenting that you would write, but you forgot the flash drive with your book on it at home, consider saving your book to the cloud so it's accessible everywhere and impossible to leave behind. Or, if your issue is that you can't use this writing time because your laptop is too big to lug everywhere, get a Bluetooth keyboard so you can write on your phone or tablet. If distractions are the obstacle, noise-canceling headphones or an internet block might be just the thing.

Make it easy for you to write. When you eliminate the roadblocks to writing, you limit your excuses for not getting it done. When it's easier to write than to come up with a good reason not to, that's when you'll get it done more times than not.

Motivation

Dorothy Parker famously said, "I hate writing, I love having written."

Turns out, writing isn't always fun! And while you don't have to write every single day, you do have to keep working at it regularly if you want to reach your goals. How do you keep getting the words down and building up your writing habit on those days when the last thing you feel like doing is writing?

Motivation is a tricky beast and a very personal thing. I was recently part of a writing challenge with a tight deadline and a high word count goal. When I saw that huge goal, I thought, "Challenge accepted!" stretched my fingers and then wrote my butt off for weeks to try to hit it. I didn't know if I'd be able to achieve the target in time, but having that difficult goal motivated me to give it my all and write more than I would have otherwise. I ended up hitting the target and writing twice as much as I planned, making it a very productive month.

But that same goal discouraged scores of others. The forums were full of writers for whom it was so large and overwhelming it seemed impossible to hit, so why even try? That same goal that spurred me to do more than I thought I could did the exact opposite for them. They quit, frustrated.

If you know what works for you, it's a great idea to start collecting tricks you know you can use to motivate yourself in a pinch. Little things that work to help you keep up your writing habit and making forward progress on your writing goals even when your enthusiasm is flagging. I'm a big believer in using whatever it takes to keep you motivated, even if it feels silly, so experiment and see how it goes.

While you know yourself best and may already have some ideas, let me share some things that worked for me.

Keep track of your writing progress

In 2009, I knew I wasn't writing as much as I would like and I was trying to figure out how to build up a more consistent writing habit when I realized: I actually had no idea how much or how often I was already writing. How would I know if I was improving if I had nothing to compare it to? So I started to keep a record of how much I wrote each day.

It ended up being the most powerful thing I've ever done to build my writing habit. And it could not have been simpler.

While I used an electronic spreadsheet (using the free Google Sheets to be specific), you can also keep a simple paper record. I only opted for electronic because cloud saving ensured I had it with me at all times, and then I had the data accessible to analyze and make into charts. (Yes, this is the part where I out myself as a huge nerd.)

Every time I wrote, I logged those words toward the total word count for that day. At first, I only kept a record of word count, but I later expanded it to include time spent writing and other metrics. You could also do this by page count, number of lines, or whatever measure you prefer to track writing with.

Over time, this spreadsheet got more complex so I could track multiple projects, genres, fiction vs. non-fiction, and more. I also built in space to leave myself notes about how each writing session went and what I was working on that day. A friend peeked over my shoulder when I was logging my daily writing and asked me if I was running the stock market from that thing because, over the years, it's gotten pretty complex.

But I didn't have any of that in the beginning. At the start, it was only a bare-bones record of how much I had written and when. Which is why I was amazed when it had an immediate and drastic change in my writing habits.

You wouldn't think keeping track would increase the amount you write, but it turns out that being accountable to something, even if that something is a spreadsheet no one looks at but you, makes you more likely to keep at it. And once you have your numbers in front of you like that, they motivate you too. You think, "Surely, I can at least write more than I did yesterday..." or "Hmm, only 500 more words and this will be my biggest word count week ever! Might as well go for it!" and before you know it, you're getting competitive even though your only opponent is Past You.

But even if you aren't competitive, there are other reasons to keep track of how much and how often you write. Having that data to refer back to can help you find patterns in how you work and refine your writing process over time. It can also help you set realistic goals and deadlines because you know your typical writing speed.

Having somewhere to log how much you wrote each day makes the writing feel real and more important than when you're not even keeping track. And, most of all, it serves as a reminder of what you've accomplished so far. It's pretty darn satisfying to watch those totals go up up up over a week, a year, a lifetime. I can't tell you how many months I've felt like I'm a failure who hasn't accomplished anything, but before I can wallow in that funk, I pull up my spreadsheet and, huh, turns out I'd been writing a lot more than I thought I did.

So even if you aren't a numbers nerd, start keeping a record of how much you wrote, when you wrote it and what you were working on. Not only will it help you have a sense of how your efforts to build a writing life are going, but it will also increase your productivity and confidence at the same time. Not to mention that when writing accolades and big deals are still far away, it will give you plenty of small milestones to celebrate!

Weekly, monthly and yearly goals

Another great way to build a writing habit is to set goals and deadlines for yourself. While some writers set a daily goal, my life is far too unpredictable for that. Instead, I like to set monthly and yearly goals. That way there's wiggle room and the flexibility to take a week off or catch up as needed depending on my schedule.

The best goals are challenging but still doable. Flexible enough that you can take days off but still tight enough that you won't waste a whole week on one sentence. Start small, both in terms of your how much you plan to write and in the period you set the goal for, until you have a better sense of your writing pace. You can always change or adjust it later. If you know your average words or page per minute and the amount of time you have to write per day, you can multiply your way to a custom goal tailored to your exact situation.

If you've never set a writing goal of any kind before or you don't have enough data yet to know your typical writing speed, I recommend starting with about 100,000 words for the year. That works out to just over 250 words a day, a very doable amount even if you only have a few minutes to write, and easy to make up if you miss a day. It's also just about the length of most traditionally published novels, so it gives you a meaningful target to shoot for even if you're not writing a novel. The equivalent would be about 8,000 words for the month.

Having both short and long term word count goals helps you stay on track and solidifies your writing habit. It's the steady progress over the long term that will lead to meaningful progress on your goals. And I fully endorse making writing goals more fun to chase by celebrating or getting yourself rewards when you hit that target!

Streaks and chains

A straightforward and popular motivational method that lends itself to writing is the streak. With a streak, you try to hit your goal every day, so you don't break the chain. For example, every day you write, you mark that day off on your calendar with a big x or special sticker. If you keep this up, you'll have a long chain of days marked off, and then the pressure to not break that streak helps keep you going in the days ahead.

While you'd typically measure a streak daily, you can set your own streak parameters however you want. Maybe only weekdays count so you can take weekends off without ruining your streak. Perhaps you have to hit a minimum word or page count for that day to count for the chain. Or your streak could be weekly, tracking weeks you wrote something like at least 3 days or 1,000 words, to give you some flexibility.

The idea is to motivate you to come up with a regular schedule and stick to it. The more days you take off, the more likely you are to keep taking days off. Objects in motion stay in motion, and it's a lot harder to get started again once you stop. Trying to keep a streak alive is another way to help keep you focused on building up that writing habit until it feels second nature.

Gamification and gimmicks

Gamification refers to turning anything into a game. There is only one game I know of specifically for writing, 4TheWords, a fantasy-style game where you battle monsters, collect items and progress in quests all by writing, but there are dozens of other productivity systems not tailored explicitly to writing that you can adapt. There is a Don't Break the Chain app for tracking writing streaks. HabitRPG lets you turn any your daily tasks into a fantasy type game. 750words offers badges and other rewards for checking in to write every day.

Sure, they are gimmicks, but sometimes they can be very effective at motivating. I started on 4TheWords during a time when I was in a real writing slump postpartum, and it turned out to be the perfect thing to trick my overtired brain into making writing progress again. Making a game of your writing goals can make the process more fun and give you little victories to celebrate while you're still far from bigger writing glories.

Deadlines (self-imposed)

So many people say they will write a book "someday." But if they don't sit down and circle a date on the calendar to be that someday will it happen? Keep yourself motivated and writing regularly by setting a deadline for each stage of your writing project.

Setting a deadline means picking a specific date and committing to finishing your writing project by that date. Math is your friend for setting a realistic deadline. If you know you need to write 50,000 more words to finish this draft and you write about 500 words a day, then your deadline should be at least 100 days out from today's date.

[words to write] / [your average # of words a day] = [the minimum # of days away the deadline should be]

I say the minimum number of days because it's always a good idea to build in some wiggle room for unforeseen complications and emergencies (and for taking a night off once in a while!) so tack on a few extra days. But just as with setting overall writing goals, you want a deadline challenging enough that it takes steady writing to reach it in time, but is still realistic based on your typical writing output.

It can be tricky to get your brain to take a deadline you set yourself seriously. Writing it down helps so note the deadline and various benchmarks along the way on your calendar or daily planner. Some people like to record their target word or page count for each day to keep them on track while others just note the significant milestones (10,000 words, 25,000 words, etc.). Posting your deadline where you can't miss it (or making it your background image) can also ensure you don't forget about it.

Another easy way to make it feel real is to designate a prize for completing the project on time. This works best when you know exactly what the award will be and you've got a picture of it tacked up somewhere to keep you focused on achieving it. You can reward yourself for hitting your deadline by buying yourself a present you've had your eye on, having a special night out or by waiting to enjoy a book, video game or movie until after you're finished. Alternately, if your brain works better the other way around, a punishment for missing your deadline might be to donate to a politician you despise or tackle a dreaded household chore.

One reason I love the NaNoWriMo.org writing challenges is that they give you that feeling of having an external deadline with no negative consequences if you miss it, only lovely prizes if you do.

Deadlines (external)

So long as they aren't expensive to submit to and don't have weird rights grabs or other sketchy publication terms, it's never a bad idea to get more of your writing out there to build up your portfolio and increase your skills. Browse upcoming writing contests, anthology calls, and other submission opportunities and use their due dates as deadlines either to finish something you've been working on a while or to start something new just for that opportunity. This gives you a hard deadline that feels real but in a low stakes setting where missing the deadline isn't a big deal since the judges never knew to expect your entry anyway.

While there are contests for book-length work or excerpts from novels, this trick works best for short stories, personal essays, 10-minute plays, and other smaller writing projects. I've gotten so many things out the door I otherwise would have left unfinished because I wanted to submit them to some anthology or contest opportunity and the deadline gave me that push to finally finish them. Even if you aren't the lucky winner, you've still completed something that you can always use for future opportunities and have the satisfaction of taking something all the way to completion.

Silly Self-Challenges

While a deadline can work great for getting that one specific project done, what if you're just generally looking to write more or juggling a bunch of projects? You can give yourself any writing challenge you want to dream up, no matter how silly it may seem. If it motivates you to keep writing or pushes you to do more than you thought you could, that's all that matters.

I am the queen of giving myself ridiculous self-challenges with the silliest names. During the one I called "YES-vember!" I challenged myself to write three books in 30 days (one of which was this one). During "Where There's a Will There's a MAY," I tried to write 100,000 words in a single month (May, obviously). When I lost the first two weeks of March to illness, I tried to get caught up on my writing goals within the last two weeks with, "In Like a Lion, Out like a BAM!".

I have given myself challenges based on the month, season, or random days of the weeks. I have set up challenges from the number of stories I send out to what percentage of my writing was fiction vs. non-fiction. My current dare is to read at least two plays a month to help me better understand the market I write for. (I call this one, "The Play's the Thing!" if you were wondering!)

Sometimes I set a self-challenge because I need to motivate myself to do the work that needs to be done, but, lots of times, I'm just making my own fun and want to see what I am capable of. And, yes, the silly names are essential because they help these challenges feel special by setting them aside from the writing work I'm already doing every day. They also give me a fun thing to bellow when my loved ones ask me what I'm working on.

If you find yourself musing, "I wonder if I could...?" Do it! Challenge yourself and see what you can accomplish. And if you fail, no one else will have known about it anyway and keeping it silly ensures it won't hurt too much if you fall short.

Finish What You Start

Consider yourself warned: There's a point, usually around the halfway point of your story but not always, when you will hit a moment of crisis. *This story is a mess, my writing is awful, the characters are flat and dull, and the whole thing is falling apart. Why am I even bothering to write this?* This feeling will often coincide with the siren call of a shiny new idea that would be sooo much easier to write, and it'll try to convince you that maybe you should just go write that and stop wasting your time with this disaster.

When you hit this point, it will feel very personal, rooted in all your fears and insecurities, but it's a universal experience. From Stephen King to J. K. Rowling, all writers have talked about this dark moment when it feels like their story, their draft, nay, their entire writing career unravels. But what the experienced writer knows that the new one doesn't is that this is not a sign to quit or chase your latest plot bunny to a new story, but a normal part of the process. The only way out is through. Keep writing past this pocket of doom, and you'll find your footing again on the other side.

There was a point in every single thing I've ever written where I ended up sobbing to my husband that the story doesn't work and I'm a complete failure and I have no idea how to write and all my successes so far have been a fluke and--- Oh, wait, never mind, I've got it!

And then I'm right back to it.

Finish what you start. If the story was worth starting, it's worth finishing. Jot down ideas for that shiny new idea, so you don't forget it but then get your butt back in the chair and get back to work.

Middles are hard. It's when the novelty of the new project has worn off, and the narrative gets tricky. It's also when you've been writing for long enough that it's stopped being fun and you're just looking for an out. But the good news is that, as hard as middles are, endings are easier. Push through the murky middle, and you'll find yourself flying again, you and your story accelerating through the climax to the end.

There are some things you can only learn about a project (and about writing itself) from taking something all the way to its conclusion. It's easy to chase the latest shiny new idea, but it's by doing the hard work of finishing what you start that will level up your skills and give you a finished project you can do something with.

Set better goals

In the first section, we talked about turning your writing dreams into writing goals. But anyone can look at the failure rate of New Year's Resolutions to realize most of us are terrible at setting goals. We set ourselves up for failure by being inflexible or aiming too high, we set goals that are too vague, we chase things we think we should want instead of what we actually want and we try to tackle the whole project at once instead of breaking it down into manageable pieces. Rather than put ourselves through all the misery of a bad goal, it's a good idea to make sure the writing goals we're setting for ourselves are specific, realistic, flexible and what we really want.

Realistic

Some writers think managing their expectations means compromising their dreams, but I don't see it that way. Because if you're serious about getting that ultimate, pie-in-the-sky vision of what you want for you and your writing, you know you've got to start somewhere, right? Acknowledging that something is out of your reach right now, doesn't negate the fact that you may reach it later on.

If you average 1,000 words an hour but only have thirty minutes of writing time a day, it's not realistic to expect yourself to write 10,000 words a week. The math just doesn't work out. In the same way, if it's your very first time writing ever, it's not realistic to expect an agent to throw a six-figure book deal at you at their first peek of your first draft. You've got some work to do before you get there.

Keep yourself from getting discouraged and frustrated early on by setting realistic goals. You know how much time you have to write, your average words per minute, your current skill level. Use this knowledge to set challenging but realistic goals that are doable within the context of who you are as a writer right now. You can always adjust over time as your circumstances change and skills increase.

Flexible

Part of being realistic is flexibility. Things will happen, life will get in the way, and things won't go quite as planned. If your goal can roll with the unplanned, you have a better chance of righting yourself whenever you get derailed.

Build in breaks for yourself! Leave a little breathing room! We're all impatient to see our dreams realized, but if you set a goal that's so rigid you can never take a night off to take care for yourself, you'll burn out before you get to see it through. Flexibility means setting a goal that fits into your life and acknowledging the reality that sometimes things come up.

It's also about being malleable to the changes in your writing career and the publishing industry. Think about me so convinced that I had to write novels or nothing that I missed dozens of opportunities for writing plays right under my nose. You can stay focused on what you want but still flexible enough to take a chance you didn't plan for if it comes up.

People get this way about publishing, convinced that only self or traditional publishing is for them and refusing to consider any other option. I've self-published and had traditional publishing deals. I reevaluate which is the best path to take for this specific project every time I finish something. This is an industry in flux, and it doesn't make sense to limit my opportunities by ignoring any one publication option in favor of another.

Be flexible. You know the expression in nature that says, "Adapt or perish"? While it doesn't have to be as dramatic as all that, staying nimble and open to change or challenge can make you that much more likely to meet your goals.

Specific

But the biggest rookie mistake people make when setting goals is leaving them too vague. The more specific a goal is, the easier it is for you to take direct action towards achieving it. The best goals are well defined with clear, actionable steps. That means "finish the first draft of a 150-page book by August 4th" is a much better goal than "write a book this summer."

Let's take a common writing goal: write a bestseller. Well, what the heck does that mean? Because it could mean that you want to get an agent and then a traditional publishing deal and then have that book be a big enough success that it hits the New York Times bestseller list, the holy grail of publishing. That path could mean writing dozens to hundreds of books in the service of finding first an agent then an editor and then that elusive book that gets just the right marketing push and connects with readers enough to hit the bestseller list.

Or it could mean that you want to self-publish a single book and have it hit one of Amazon's various bestseller lists for each genre, a task that's not that hard to achieve with the right balance of keywords, ads, and marketing.

Remember when I asked you what you really wanted from your writing? The more you nailed that down, the easier it will be for you to set a specific goal for achieving it and take real, concrete steps towards the target.

Goals within goals: Break it down

Here's the thing about setting goals that trips people up: Big goals are made up of lots of smaller goals. Those small goals, in turn, are made up of even tinier goals (I call these tasks). To accomplish any of your big writing goals, you need to first think small.

Imagine sitting down to write and the only item on your to-do list for the night is "Write Book." In fact, that's been the only item on the list for months because it takes a very long time to write a book all the way from start to finish so you never even get the satisfaction of crossing that item off. The whole project still looms ahead of you, and no matter how much you've accomplished so far, your to-do list looks the same every day because you still aren't able to cross "Write Book" off your list.

Now consider that you sit down to write, but, this time, your to-do list reads "write 500 words" or "research dentures in the 1600s" or "revise page 10." You see right away how these are less overwhelming? Any one of those tasks is finite and small enough that you could accomplish it in a single writing session. Then you could have the satisfaction of crossing it off the list and moving to the next thing. But each of these small tasks still represents progress you're making on your big goal of writing a book.

This is a complicated idea to wrap your head around at first but essential to making real progress on your most ambitious dreams. In the next part, we'll go more in-depth with how this process would work in real life. Once you understand the basic idea, you'll discover it's a great way to break down all your big projects, even the ones that have nothing to do with writing. If this is more goal setting nerdery than you're ready for, feel free to skip ahead to the next section.

Nested goals

The hierarchy of goals goes like this...

- Ultimate Goal
- Project Goals
- Secondary Goals
- Tasks

You want something from your writing life. Let's call this your Ultimate Goal. But the road to getting there is paved with lots of smaller goals, let's call them Project Goals. Project Goals can be individual stories or books you want to write, or they can be other things to help your career such as "Build an Author Website," "Query Agents" or "Advertise Freelance Services." A Project Goal is really just a way of organizing everything you need to do to accomplish something all in one place. Some Project Goals will be so complex they might take several years to fully complete, and others will be for shorter projects that only take a few days or weeks.

Those Project Goals are, in turn, made up of Secondary Goals. Secondary Goals are like milestones, big steps with clear ending points that all take you closer to completing the Project Goal. Then each Secondary Goal breaks down into the tiniest goal unit of all: the Task. Tasks are the little steps you take day to day that get you closer to completing your Secondary Goal.

Nest Goals Example

Let's say your Ultimate Goal is to become a published author. What's the first thing you'd need to do to get closer to that Ultimate Goal? Write a book. Thus "Write a Book" becomes your first Project Goal.

But that's not specific enough to be a good goal so we break that Project Goal down into as many Secondary Goals as we can think of. What are the significant steps and milestones to writing a book? For this example, Secondary Goals for writing a book might be

- Research and Develop Idea
- Outline
- Complete First Draft
- Revise into the Second Draft
- Polish for Beta Readers
- Revise based on Beta Reader Feedback

... and so on based on the publication path you choose.

From there, you can break down the first Secondary Goal into the specific Tasks needed to complete it. In other words, list every single step you can think of it would take to be able to cross that Secondary Goal off your list. Don't worry if you can't think of everything right now, you'll inevitably end up changing and adding Tasks as you go. Ideally, you should size each of these Tasks so they should only take a single writing session to complete.

For "Complete First Draft," for example, these Tasks may be a list of all the scenes you plan to include in your book or, if you're not a planner, a list of Tasks such as "write 500 words" or "write 1 page" over and over to tally up your word or page count goal for that draft. For "Research and Develop Idea" it might be a list of questions you know to look up the answers to, links to read or characters to figure out. Your Task list for "Revise into the Second Draft" may include things like, "Change Chapter 4 to past tense" or "add more tension to the doctor scene."

The day you've checked off every single Task you can think of under your Secondary Goal is the day it's finished, and you can move on to the next one! In most cases, you won't be able to break down the next Secondary Goal into Tasks until you've completed the Secondary Goal before it. For instance, you probably won't know how to revise your book into the second draft until you finish your first draft.

Every time you complete one of those Tasks, you bring yourself another step closer to completing that Secondary Goal which, in turn, will complete a big chunk of your Project Goal and also represents a significant step forward in achieving your Ultimate Goal. Over a whole writing life, you will have many Project Goals all designed to get you closer to that Ultimate Goal, each of them broken down into Secondary Goals and Tasks you can work on daily. And thus, day by day, you bring yourself closer and closer to achieving your goals.

Goals nested within goals all the way down. It may sound overwhelming written this way but, when you sit down to do it, it's actually both calming and remarkably motivating. The point is to break a massive and overwhelming project down to individual tasks that are small enough that it feels manageable. It's thinking ahead about what it will take to achieve what you want and then organizing those thoughts in both the big picture and daily details.

There's something about taking what was this huge amorphous project and breaking it down and down again until it's a harmless little list of tasks. It lays a roadmap at your feet, so you know you only need to do x then y then z and you'll have reached your goal. It lets you ignore the enormity of your Master Plan and, instead, just focus on doing something today that will eventually add up to something amazing. It's also very satisfying to get to cross at least one little thing off your list each writing day and know you're making progress on all your bigger goals at the same time.

The other good thing about breaking a big project down this way is that, when you reach the end of a Secondary Goal, there's the opportunity to bask in the progress you've made so far. You are absolutely entitled to a break and/or reward every time you complete a Secondary Goal before you dive into the next one. This is a lot mentally healthier and means little celebrations and breaks every few weeks instead of only celebrating at the very end when you finish the whole big Project Goal maybe years down the line.

You can do this same process with any writing project, even ongoing projects like keeping a journal or smaller works with a quick turnaround time like a freelance article. Just adjust the goals and tasks accordingly. Take your larger goals and figure out how to break them down into smaller bits.

Get started by brainstorming. What are the big things you want to accomplish that would get you closer to your Ultimate Goal? How can you break each of those Project Goals down into Secondary Goals, aka distinct milestones with definite endpoints? And then, exactly what is everything you would you need to do to cross off that first Secondary Goal? That's your list of Tasks you'll work on day to day until you run out and the Secondary Goal is complete. Then you'll repeat that process as you reach the next Secondary Goal and then the next until the Project Goal is done.

Go big by thinking small. Think of it as eating a big apple bite by bite instead of trying to shove it all into your mouth at once. While it can feel unnatural to slow down and organize your thoughts when you're filled with big ideas, remember that you undertake even the longest journey step by step.

Back-up your work!

There's another critical step you have to make part of your writing routine that's very easy to overlook. No matter how you write, no matter where you write, make sure you always back up your work! Computers die, files get corrupted and overwritten, stuff gets stolen. It's bad enough when a crisis hits, you don't want to lose all your hard work too!

While many writing programs back-up automatically every few minutes, it's a good idea to also back them up with another method as an additional safety measure. Whether you use an automatic cloud back-up like Dropbox or Google Drive or just email a copy of your book to yourself at the end of every writing session, making sure there is always at least one other copy of your work somewhere else is an easy way to avoid disaster. Make a dated back-up of everything before making any changes so previous versions are easy to find. This way, when you are inevitably revising something and end up making it worse (Hey, we've all been there!), you've still got the old version to work with.

I know, I sound paranoid but it's so easy to get lazy about back-ups until the worst happens to you and it's too late.

Back-up early. Back-up often. Set yourself a reminder if you have to. Trust me on this.

Privacy and protection

In this digital age, privacy is something everyone should worry about, but how does it pertain to writing? Do you really want just anyone reading what you wrote until it's ready or maybe ever if it's something very personal? Most cloud back-up solutions have some kind of password protection but nothing more. Do you need stronger protections like encryption or a decryption key?

If your writing isn't online in the first place, no one can access it no matter how many ways hackers attack. This is a significant perk to writing in a paper notebook or only on your local computer, bypassing the internet and cloud entirely. If you do opt for offline writing, make sure you set up a back-up option such as an external hard drive or series of flash drives so you won't lose your work if something happens to your original copy.

But is only writing offline realistic? These days it's almost impossible to keep your writing entirely off the internet. You'll have to email it or save it to the cloud eventually, especially if you are eying publication. So how can you make sure it's protected once you do?

Password protection

One of the simplest things you can do to protect your work is also the one most people overlook because of pure laziness: You need strong passwords that you do not reuse on more than one site, and you need to remember to change them often. So simple and yet I'm sure you can think of at least one old password you've been using for ages on a dozen sites, putting yourself and your data at risk just because it's familiar.

You absolutely need robust, unique passwords on all the following...

- The program you write in (if it has a login feature, which many do not)
- Your cloud-based back-up or storage system
- Your email address... because that's where any password reset emails will go. Anyone can undo your entire online security if they can access your email because it's where most password resets go.

If your passwords are all strong, fresh and unique (i.e., you're not using the same password on multiple sites), and your virus and spyware detection software is up to date and running regular scans, that is likely all the protection the average person needs. It's also a good idea to get in the habit of always logging in directly from the official website and never trusting links sent in email or text since that's one of the easiest ways scammers steal your passwords. Keep in mind that the average scammer is much more interested in your banking details or identity so they can turn a quick buck, not your writing ideas. As long as you keep your online identity and data as safe as you can, your writing is safe too.

Your words are copyrighted as soon as you write them so, even if someone did steal your work, they wouldn't be able to do anything with it. A lot of writers worry about this because they are sure everyone will want to steal their million-dollar best-selling idea and, if this is your main concern, you can breathe easy. We all like to think we are the most exceptional untapped talent of the modern era, but, the truth is, ideas are cheap. Unless you're already a household name where everyone is desperate to get your latest work, your ideas are safe.

What I do think is worth being worried about is more personal writing, such as journaling, where you might divulge sensitive information that would put you at risk for embarrassment, identity theft, and other scams.

Encrypting your writing

If you want to make sure absolutely no one but you can read something, you must encrypt it. What is encryption? It's a process that scrambles the data, in this case, your text, so it is unreadable unless you have a specific password or decryption key. Sometimes, this key or password changes daily or even hourly for maximum security.

Problem is, what makes encryption so safe is also its biggest downside: lose the key or password, and even you won't be able to access your own data. It's scrambled for good and as good as gone. That said, so far, no encryption is truly unbreakable, so there's almost always a way to hack your way back in with enough tech expertise. But that can mean a hassle of delays and extra costs on your end and also sort of defeats the purpose.

There are dozens of encryption services out there that let you protect your data no matter what your platform or writing program. A few of the popular journaling sites and software offer a level of encryption as part of their base service but not enough of them, and it's usually all or nothing. OneNote lets you encrypt individual pages or notebooks and leave others open which can be a good compromise solution.

Overall, when it comes to your writing, be smart and safe online, but you don't need to be too paranoid about people accessing it without your permission. If an extra measure of protection would let you worry less and write more, it's worth it to add. But if you are attentive about your passwords and smart about your data online, that's likely all you need.

Habit Forming

Building a writing habit is not about this one year or even writing this one story. It's a lifetime commitment to words and stories. It's understanding that, when you started writing, it was the first day of the rest of your life. Your writing life.

And you're really doing it now! You know that the writing itself is the thing. You've integrated writing into your life and woven it into your routine, so it's as natural as breathing. You've built up consistency with your writing and are doing the steady work of moving closer to your goals. You have the solid base that you need to keep building your writing life.

If the foundation of a building isn't sound, it doesn't matter what you build on top. Your foundation holds everything else up, no matter how high you build your dreams, and keeps you steady in a storm. And, most importantly, it's made to last.

At this point, you're realizing that writing is not always daydreams and gumdrops. If you're in this for the long haul of seeing your goals through to the end, it will take dedication, motivation, and a heck of a lot of work. But it's that solid writing habit you've taken the time to build that will sustain you and hold you up for all the work ahead.

In this section, you built up a writing habit by...

- Writing regularly without worrying if it's every day.
- Wrote even when not inspired.
- Removed obstacles and excuses, making it easier to get the words down.
- Motivated yourself when the going got hard with writing statistics, goals, silly challenges, streaks, gamification, and other gimmicks.
- Finished what you started, no matter how much you doubted yourself or got distracted by a shiny new idea.

- Set flexible, realistic, and specific goals.
- Broke bigger goals down into smaller goals and then again into daily tasks you could complete in a single writing session.
- Got into the habit of backing up often to avoid disaster and losing all your work!
- Protected your work and kept it private with encryption, stronger passwords, and sensible online safety practices.

Look at that foundation! Sure, it might be a little boring and gray, but it's solid, dependable, and ready to hold up whatever you do next. Now that we've got some structure to this writing life, it's time to get the walls and other essential bits up so you can finally move in.

MOVE IN

Discover Your Writing Process

By now, you've been working on building your writing life, and you've got something solid, dependable, and real. You're mentally committed to being a writer. You've started writing, and you've built up a regular writing habit. You can stop and look around at what you've built and realize... you've really got something here. Something built to last and ready for whatever you decide to do. And that's exciting.

Now it's time to move in. Arrange the furniture just how you like it, paint the walls your favorite colors, make it comfortable. You've made a place for writing in your life, so let's make it yours.

Writing is an incredibly personal process. There are no two people alike, and no two writers get their words down the same way. What works for me may not work for you, and that's fine.

What, where, when, and how do you like to write? Your personal set of writing preferences, the things you know work best for you and your writing, add up to your writing process. You'll be fine-tuning and discovering things about your process for the rest of your life. And the more you understand about your writing process, the more comfortable you can make it on yourself to keep writing and moving forward with your writing goals.

You've probably started to realize a few things already. What's been working well so far? What hasn't? Maybe your attempt at Morning Pages was a disaster, and you've realized Night Notes are a better fit for your natural rhythms. Or perhaps that fancy writing software left you overwhelmed and wordless, but your story flows quick and easy whenever you open your good old paper notebook.

Whatever works for you, embrace it, even if it goes against conventional wisdom. The point of figuring out your writing process is to find your personal path of least resistance to getting the words down. But whether you feel you've already found your writing groove or everything is still mostly a mystery, let's talk about some strategies for fine-tuning your writing process for a more satisfying and productive writing life.

In this section, you'll break down your writing process to help build your best writing life. You'll identify what writing advice you should try and which you can ignore and then work on understanding what and how you like to write and where you prefer to do it. Then you'll examine when you write, diving into a wealth of tricks for both finding and making more writing time, and taking the best advantage of the time you have. Lastly, you'll tap into the motivating power of your ideal writing circumstances and share strategies for capturing that magic when those circumstances aren't available.

As you go through this section, jot down what you know so far about how you prefer to write and consider new angles. Think about the questions I pose. It will all help you get a better picture of your writing process that you can both refer to and refine. Keep in mind that these are all just suggestions and things you can experiment with.

As you figure out which ones work for you and which ones don't, that all helps to give you a clearer picture of your personal writing process.

So, grab that stack of decorating magazines and paint swatches and let's make this place look like home!

Taking (and ignoring) writing advice

In his books about writing craft (which have colorful language but I highly recommend), author Chuck Wendig talks about testing all writing advice against what you already know works for you. In his words, "Tell all writing advice: 'NOW YOU MUST FIGHT THE BEAR.'"

The bear in this scenario is how you are comfortable working now. If you try out the new advice and it can't defeat the bear, i.e., it doesn't work better than what you are already doing, then no matter how highly it comes recommended, you can ignore it. So soak up all the writing advice you can and give the stuff that looks good a try (because sometimes a small tweak can end up being a total game-changer), but feel free to toss it if it doesn't work for you.

This may seem simple enough, but it's harder than you'd think. As creatures of habit, we often get so set in our ways we're not willing to even try something new. We're afraid, or maybe even a little lazy, about bringing a challenger to the bear even though a better way of doing things might be right under our noses. Step out of your comfort zone and try new writing techniques, particularly when stuck. If it doesn't work for you, you can always go back to the old way but, if it does, you may have a whole new trick up your sleeve for the next time you need to change things up.

When you are a new writer, it's very tempting to take every bit of writing advice you hear as gospel, especially when you hear it from a writer you admire. But few things will serve you better throughout your writing life than to remember that everyone works differently, and it is fine if this strategy everyone else swears by isn't for you. There is no single right way of writing, and it'll never do you wrong to remember that.

Seek out new perspectives on writing from your peers, craft books, blog posts, and articles. Never stop learning and experimenting. It can't hurt to have something extra in your writing toolbox for when the going gets tough. But don't lose sight of the fact that the best advice in the world is worthless if you cannot make it work for you.

Your writing wheelhouse

There comes the point in every writer's life when they sit back and look at all the words they've accumulated throughout their writing life and notice some patterns. Many of us return to not just the same genres but also the same character types, themes, and tropes again and again. Don't worry, this isn't a bad thing! Publishers and readers like when their favorite authors write things very much like that other thing of theirs they already know they like.

There is undeniable power in starting to understand your literary wheelhouse, especially when you know your audience digs it too, but you don't have to let it limit you. Never forget that you can write whatever you want. Nothing limits you to just one type of writing, one genre, one format, fiction or non. In fact, experimenting and widening the scope of what you write can not only sharpen your writing skills across the board but also increase your chances of success.

Just as it takes more than one punch to break through a wall, it can take many different projects before you finally get it, whether that "it" is a publishing target or better understanding of a concept. If you feel weird about branching out, I recommend the freeing feeling of writing under a pen name. Whether or not you keep it secret, knowing a different name is on the byline can free you up in ways you can't imagine.

Similarly, if a writing project isn't working, try it in another format. Convert that novel into a screenplay, that personal essay to fiction. Switching formats can help you see the story from a new perspective and sometimes even find a better way through. Maybe it'll work better the new way! Even if it doesn't, another genre or format can teach you new writing tricks you can bring back to the original.

Being a writer is a lot like being a shark. You never stop moving, the urge to write pushing you forward. Use it! When you finish one thing, write the next and then the next. All the while, you'll be leveling up your skills and, if the first thing falls through, you've already got something else ready to go.

Where do you write?

Some writers love the buzz of a busy coffee shop. Others prefer to curl up under the covers and write in bed. Some swear by that certain spot on the couch that they've worn into a perfectly comfortable groove.

While I'm in favor of getting used to writing just about anywhere, I also know I get my best writing done when I'm in my usual spot where everything is just where I expect it. If you've already found your perfect writing spot, great! But if you're still trying to find that place, here are some things to consider.

Get your own space.

If you've got the space to make a study or have a huge ponderous writing desk, having a sacred space for writing can minimize distractions, help you focus, and increase both your productivity and creativity. But if you don't have a whole room to spare, you can still make yourself a designated writing space with a little creativity. Many writers have turned all or part of a closet into a small desk space (my dad used one for years). Some desks fold or slide out or even roll away when not being used. If you have the space to do the writing, that space needn't be permanent or big so long as it does the job.

Let a space fill a double-duty.

I know many writers who use their kitchen or dining room table as their writing desk. They set their laptops up on the table to write and then tuck everything away come mealtime. My "standing desk" is my bedroom vanity with my laptop on it. Stephen King used to write on the lid of a washing machine. If you can be an accountant by day, writer by night, there's no reason any surface can't do the same double-duty!

Get comfy.

Sometimes the simple act of getting physically comfortable can make you more mentally comfortable to write. There's a big reason a lot of writers write in bed, snuggled in their PJs. If you have trouble getting out from under the covers in the morning for an early writing session, you may as well move the writing session into bed with you!

Get out of the house.

A change in scenery can bring a shift in perspective and an escape from the distractions at home, ranging from dirty dishes to raucous roommates. With a laptop or mobile writing set-ups like a Bluetooth keyboard and tablet or smartphone, it's easy to take your writing on the go. Whether you opt for somewhere industrious, like a shared office space where everyone else is also working diligently, or somewhere inspiring like a pretty park, having somewhere to go to write can make it feel more real like a regular job and make you more likely to take it seriously.

Coffee shops are notorious havens for writers, but you could just as easily set up shop at a table in a diner or bar if that's more your speed. Libraries also usually have a section with comfy chairs or desks, and at least you know it'll be quiet there. I know writers who've done "write-ins" on trains, in malls, in the middle of the woods and even in theme parks just to get a change of scenery.

Think ergonomically.

If the physical act of writing becomes painful or uncomfortable, rethink where you write to make it more ergonomic. While it's relaxing to curl up on the couch, it can hurt to type that way after a while. There are a variety of repetitive stress injuries you can give yourself from writing by hand, typing, and even sitting for any length of time. Think of your back, your joints (fingers, wrists, elbows) and even your eyes which can get strained from staring at a monitor too long or writing in dim lighting. Find a place to write that works for your body and mind.

But if you still can't find that special writing spot, never fear! When you get into the writing zone, your surroundings tend to melt away until it's just you alone with the words. Once you're transported to the world of your story, it may not matter to you that much where you parked your body.

How do you craft a story?

While you may not have this all figured out yet, a big part of your writing process is understanding how you prefer to craft the stories themselves. Are you a writer that hops around, writing scenes as they come to you, or do you need to start from the beginning and write in order? Do you like the structure of formatting your scripts from the first word or do you, like me, only bother to organize them into proper play format in the final stages of the revision process? Do have every character named and fully formed in your head before you write, or do you just write and discover who they are along the way?

How you write, your preferred way of plying the writing craft, is a significant part of your writing process, and it's worth paying attention to. Knowing what you prefer and what has worked for you in the past can give you more confidence going forward and make future writing projects that much easier. But while it's important to know what you prefer, understand that you may at some point find yourself out of your writing comfort zone.

A simple example is the classic debate between plotters, people who meticulously plan and outline everything before they write, and pantsers, people who take an idea and run with it, letting the characters and story decide where it goes. You may decide that you are an avowed pantser and that the very idea of doing some planning or prep work ahead of time sounds like no fun at all. But while pantsing may be what you prefer, once you go pro, editors and publishers often require an outline or synopsis of the whole project before they'll commit, so you'll eventually have to do some plotting if that's what you want.

As you grow and change as a writer, you may also find that how you write has changed with you. As with anything, go with what is comfortable for you but stay flexible and experiment. What worked for the last story might not work for this one, and it never hurts to have an alternate strategy in your back pocket just in case.

Write with a friend. (Or not.)

Being a writer can be lonely. It's inspiring to have another writer typing along next to you, someone to keep you accountable and on task. It's also nice to have someone to talk with who understands the unique foibles of the writing life and can celebrate your victories and commiserate with your failures. Some writers rent a shared workspace so they can split the costs. Others have a standing time and location, such as a coffee shop or library, when they meet with their writing friends and get the words down together. For many writers, having their peers writing diligently around them is an essential part of staying motivated and productive.

But it's not for everyone. I love to chat with other writers, but I'm way more productive by myself. I don't mind the occasional group write-in, but I'd much rather be alone where I can blast my tunes, talk to myself, or click my pen without it bothering anyone. To me, having other writers around is more distracting than inspiring.

If you gain creative strength from having writing buddies, check out a writing group in your area or start your own weekly write-ins through Shut Up and Write (ShutUpWrite.com). It hurts nothing to give it a try. You may realize you prefer to write alone, but you may also discover that you have a greater sense of purpose and productivity with a friend writing by your side.

Writing time

Some writers swear by morning pages, the practice of getting up early in the morning and getting their writing done first thing, before they do anything else. Others are night owls, filling pages while everyone else is in bed. Then there are the ones sneaking writing in during their commute or on their lunch hour.

When you do you prefer to write?

Your ideal writing time

All writing time is not created equally. If you've started keeping stats on when and how much you write, experiment and analyze that data to figure out what time of day you're at your most productive. This is your ideal writing time.

Writing at your ideal writing time makes writing more comfortable because you're working with your natural rhythms instead of against them. It also allows you to be more productive with less time so you can make faster progress on your goals. Once you figure out your ideal writing time, block that time off and protect it like a dragon with its hoard! Rearrange your whole day around it. This sacred block of time needs to be off-limits to interruptions, appointments, and other distractions so you can concentrate on writing and nothing else.

Except that's not always realistic.

My ideal writing time is early in the day, with a fresh pot of tea beside me, sunlight streaming through my office window. Then I'm feeling bright, alert and ready to tackle whatever I've got in front of me and my writing data shows that time is worth double any other time of day I try to write in. By contrast, by evening, I am exhausted. My brain is gooey and useless after a long day, and I take twice as long to even remember what I'm doing let alone get the words out. I don't do my best writing at night at all.

But the evening is the only time I have to write, so that's when I write. It's not ideal, and I know I could do much better writing and get a heck of a lot more done if I could block off my ideal writing time... but it's just not possible right now. So I make the most of what I've got.

It IS very good advice to figure out your ideal writing time and to keep that time scheduled, sacred and free of interruptions if you can because it will make you a happier writer and give you the best chance of reaching your writing goals. But, the fact is, circumstances are not always ideal. You may not have the luxury of lots of writing time to choose from or have a way to free up that ideal time. Sometimes all you have is this one little chunk of time you wrested away from your busy life, and it's going to have to do whether it's in line with your rhythms or not.

Get more writing time

These days, everyone's busy. I've never met a writer yet who thinks they're getting enough time to write. But we've already established that writing is important to you, so you need writing time, preferably as much as you can get.

But what if you've already booked your life solid life? What if you have no time? Chances are, there's still writing time in there somewhere but accessing it involves both finding and making time.

Find Some Time

For a week, keep track of everything you do all day, minute by minute. You can do this with paper and pen or use free apps like ManicTime or RescueTime that passively track what you're doing in the background. The idea is to account for every moment of your day and look at how you're spending your time, like an audit.

Once you have at least 7 days worth of data, look at your week. You will notice things you never realized about how you spend your time. When I first did this, I was horrified to realize how much time I wasted on social media. If you'd asked me, I'd have told you I was barely on it, just a minute here and there, but those periodic check-ins were adding up to full hours lost from my day. Maybe your vice is television or gaming or watching cat videos on YouTube, but we've all got something sucking our time that we often don't even realize we're doing that often.

There's an expression that says what you spend the most time on reflects what matters to you the most and social media doesn't matter to me as much as a lot of other things in my life, including writing. Once I limited the time I spent on social media, it freed up more time for me to do the things that did matter to me. We are creatures of habit. Often we spend time on something we don't even really like because it's what we always do when we'd be happier if we used that time up for something that matters more to us, such as working toward our writing goals. Those wasted moments can become time you can reclaim, breaking a bad habit at the same time.

But, when you audit your day, you will also notice a lot of moments when you're not doing much of anything that can become writing time too. Those fifteen minutes when you zoned out on your phone because you had to go get your kid soon so what's the point in starting something? That hour you killed on Wikipedia waiting for the wash to finish before bed. That long stretch reading random news articles while you're waiting for the bus.

While there's no shame in needing a moment to decompress and do nothing once in a while, little moments like this that you take for granted can add up into a lot of writing time, especially if you embrace the writing sprint. When you consider that the average writer can type between 500-600 words in just fifteen minutes (and that dictation is even faster than that!), you'll discover you have a lot more writing time than you think you do. Those little moments here and there can truly add up.

Make Some Time

But what if, when you audit your day, you discover there is no dead weight. Everything you're spending your time on is something that matters to you because it's essential for survival (job, cooking, etc.) or it's a leisure activity you love. You've already whittled all the downtime out of your life, and now you're wringing the most out of every second. There's just no time left to find!

If that's the case, you need to make time. And there are a few ways to go about it.

Sacrifices

Sometimes, something has to give. Maybe it's half an hour of sleep so you can get up before work or stay up a little later to get your writing done. Maybe it's cutting back on your nightly gaming session to free up time to work on your novel. Perhaps it's turning down a social engagement to stay on track with your goals.

If you're like me, your reaction to this is an immediate UGH. Because you like your life how it is, darn it, and why should you have to change it? But no one ever said reaching your goals would be easy. Sometimes you have to let go of one thing you love to make time for another.

Now, this doesn't mean cutting all joy out of your life! I'm a big believer in taking care of yourself. But it means realizing that writing and working towards your goals are significant too.

Delegate

Another way to make time, one tied inexorably with circumstances and privilege, unfortunately, is to free up more time to write by delegating something that's taking up your time. Have a relative watch your kids a few nights a week, hire someone to mow your lawn, or use a meal delivery service, so you don't have to cook. And if you're still somehow partnered with someone who isn't pulling their weight with housework or the kids, please join the rest of us in the modern era and address that immediately. Auditing your day helps you see what's taking up the most of your time. If it's something you can pay someone to do or get a friend or family to help you with, even once in a while or until you finish your project, it might well be worth the money paid or favors owed to win you back some writing time.

Here's an example from my life: With young kids, it feels like no matter how well you think you've planned, you're always running to the grocery store for something. The whole process of getting out the door, shopping, driving home in traffic, and putting away the groceries was eating up 2-3 hours of our time every week. I knew grocery pickup and delivery services existed, but I assumed they were too expensive.

When we finally took the time to look it up, do you know what our local grocery store charges to shop for us? Less than $15. And they give us a weekly coupon for $25 off which means we were wasting 2-3 hours of our life every week shopping when our grocery store would have been happy to PAY US $10 to do it for us. Now grocery shopping is a few minutes clicking off what we want on a computer and the nice people either have it ready for us to pick up at the store or drop it off at our house, and all we need to do is put it away.

I mention this because sometimes there's a thing you're doing that's taking up a lot of your time, and the solution may be simpler than you'd imagine. An app that automates that manual bookkeeping you do every week. Taking your shirts to the dry cleaner instead of doing all that washing and ironing. When it turns out that your mom was desperate for a special alone day with her beloved grandkids once a week, she just felt weird asking.

Delegate. Ask for help. Lots of times, when people know it's because you're working towards a big dream, they're more willing than usual to help. And if you can afford it, figure out the point at which your time is worth more than the money and see if there is someone (or an app or service) that you can pay to can take something off your hands.

Think outside the text box

Another way to make more writing time is to rethink what writing time is. When you get creative with how you write, the time you thought wasn't an option becomes something you can use. We have a tendency to romanticize writing as something we have to do in a ponderous study in a tweed jacket and the perfect cup of coffee, but, the fact is, as long as you are getting the words down, it doesn't matter how you did it.

Carry a small notebook with you wherever you go, so every long line or boring waiting room becomes a chance to write. Bluetooth keyboards are inexpensive and portable (some even fold or roll up to fit in your bag!) and let you type on your phone or a small tablet just about anywhere. Mobile writing can be a real game-changer, turning anything from the bus to the bathroom (Hey, I don't judge!) into a temporary writing desk.

Throw on noise-canceling headphones and write while the kids are watching Mickey Mouse Clubhouse. I have a friend who speaks out what she wants to write while her tween types it into a laptop while they drive to school, so the kid gets some typing practice while mom gets to write. Whatever works for you is fair game!

What matters is getting words down. It doesn't matter how you do it. When you rethink what writing time has to be like, you'll realize there are a lot of moments you can turn into creative space.

Especially if you don't need to use your hands at all!

Dictation

You're already talking to a startling number of devices these days, from your smart speaker to your car, but you may not realize that you can use this same technology to write using your voice. Dictation technology, also sometimes called voice-to-text, is getting better and more accurate all the time and is often faster than writing with your hands. Say the words into a microphone, and they appear on the screen like magic.

Best of all, you've likely got all the technology you need on hand right now to give dictation a try. The Windows and Apple operating systems both come with voice-to-text technology built-in that you can find under the Accessibility menu. There's also excellent free dictation software within both Google Docs (app or web browser) or Google Keyboard (mobile). With any of these options, you can get started dictating right away with the built-in microphone on your laptop or smartphone.

While the free options are great for testing and can often work surprisingly well, you'll get better and more accurate results if you upgrade your microphone, software, or both. Dragon Dictation (also sometimes called Dragon NaturallySpeaking) is the gold standard in dictation software, but it's pricey to get new, less so if you can find a used copy. Most copies of Dragon come with a free basic microphone headset that works fine but, if you want something better, prices can vary wildly. While you could use a top of the line microphone for hundreds of dollars, I've never needed anything more than the free headset Dragon came with or my lavaliere mic which cost all of $15.

Dictation means hands-free writing and makes it easier to write on the go. The more expensive editions of Dragon also give you the option to import any video recording you've done no matter what program or device you did it in, giving even you more flexibility. With voice to text, suddenly taking a long drive, doing household chores or going for a run are all opportunities to do some writing at the same time!

All that said, dictation takes some getting used to. You need to get over the hurdle of feeling awkward speaking your writing out-loud or even the sound of your own voice. But, once you are comfortable with it, dictation can rocket your writing progress forward. Because most of us speak faster than we write, you may get double the writing done in the same amount of time. It's also often easier to write a memoir, journal entries, or other more personal writing with dictation because you can just concentrate on the words. Dictation lets get your ideas directly out of your head without having to think about spelling or the rest of the actual writing process.

Keep in mind that the more you use dictation, the more you'll get used to it and the more accurate it will become as it learns your pattern of speech. Taking the time to train the software or teach it custom words can also increase its accuracy and mean fewer times you need to stop and correct. Some programs also allow you to have punctuation added automatically if you feel awkward saying, "period" or "question mark" at the end of each sentence but I've found that, over time, speaking the punctuation out loud becomes second nature just as it is while typing.

I use dictation often. I wrote almost all of this book using it. I started using it because I have joint problems and it helped me get the words down when my hands weren't cooperating with typing, but I kept using it because of how much faster it let me write. I dictate about twice as fast as I type, and I type quickly to begin with. Because I don't have a lot of writing time, dictation helps me get more done with less time, and that's a significant advantage to me. It's also handy when you have young kids because it lets you get your writing done without having to take your eyes off those little buggers!

Have you ever not felt like dealing with the little keyboard on your phone and just dictated a text to your friend? That wasn't so hard, was it? Dictating a book is just that at a much larger scale.

Make use of the little moments

"I'll be leaving soon, so there's no point in starting anything."
"He'll call any minute, so why write now only to get interrupted?"
"I've only got 15 minutes before I have to go to bed, guess I can't write today!"

Any of those sound familiar? When you fall into the trap of thinking you need some big long chunk of time to write, you ignore the small moments in your day. But those small moments can add to a lot over a whole day and making use of them is the real secret to writing around an already busy life. And when you're working on your story consistently, and it's fresh in your head, it's easy to just hop into it for a few minutes whenever you have the chance and make steady progress bit by bit.

Which is why you should master the art of the word sprint.

Word Sprints

My life is barely contained chaos between kids and work and life, and the only way I get anything written ever is because I am a great believer in the word sprint. It's a powerful little tool that can help you make the most of what writing time you have while helping you to keep making forward progress without getting overwhelmed.

Here's how it works. You set a timer for a small chunk of time. 5, 10, 15, 20 minutes... whatever you have or as long as think you can sustain focus. You start the timer and do nothing but write as much as you can until the time is up. Then you take a break. And when you have time, you do it again.

I have written almost everything I've put out since my kids were born in little chunks I wrote during sprints like these. The beauty of the word sprint is that it's so small, you've almost always got time for at least one a day. And unlike telling yourself you've got to have a three-hour typing epic which makes me tired just thinking about it, a sprint is short enough to feel doable even on those days when you're mentally and physically exhausted.

Sprints are also an easy way to break up longer writing sessions. It's a short burst of writing, followed by a break. Then you repeat as needed. Three wee writing sprints with breaks between are much easier than trying to write for an hour straight.

And here's the best part: It is amazing how much you can write in even a 15-minute sprint. Let me lay some math on you. The average person types at about 40 words per minute. That would mean you could write about 600 words in a 15-minute sprint. When you look at it that way, you could write over 200,000 words in a single year in only 15 minutes a day. That's the length of two adult novels!

Even if your typing pace is slower than average, you can still get a lot more writing than you think done by using short productive bursts of time separated by breaks. You can even adapt this technique into little Pomodoro style focus sessions for research or revision. When the whole writing project looms over you, chopping it down into short sessions with a break right each after makes it much less overwhelming and easier to conquer.

Set a timer. Write. Take a break. Repeat.

That's a word sprint, baby. And, trust me, it's a game-changer.

Different writing for different writing times

Often, when I'm doing a talk about finding and making writing time, someone comes up afterward to tell me I'm wrong. They MUST have total silence to write because ANY other sound corrupts the rhythm of their poetic voice. Or they TRIED to dictate their novel while driving and it was AWFUL so they will never use it again. Or that word sprints are a WASTE of time because their work is so research-heavy they can't accomplish ANYTHING in less than an hour.

And here's the thing: you have to do what works for you. If this one way is how you prefer it, then, yes, that's what you should do. As I've said several times now, feel free to ignore any advice that doesn't deliver better results than what you're doing now.

But I do want to make sure you realize that you don't need to write every word the same way. It takes a lot of words to be a writer, and not all of them go into your work in progress. Just because you can't make something work for one type of writing, doesn't mean it's not a viable option for writing something else.

I don't like to write plays using dictation. The dictation software doesn't cooperate with my scriptwriting software, and it's too annoying to speak out all the formatting commands. When I write a play, I type it into a good old keyboard.

But that doesn't mean I don't still use dictation for lots of other types of writing. I write non-fiction books like this, blog posts, journal entries, and answer emails almost exclusively using dictation. I also schedule my writing time accordingly. If I know I'll have a block of time at my desktop computer, I save that for typing a play, knowing I can always dictate that non-fiction chapter later when I'm watching my kids at the playground.

So maybe you find that you can't write a poem on the bus or dictate your novel while driving or sprint that big research project. That doesn't mean you can't use any of those strategies for other necessary writing like journaling, outlining, character sketches, backstory or brainstorming. Part of finding your process is realizing that some types of writing are better suited to one kind of writing time and others to another and to divide up your time with this knowledge. You can always save your ideal writing time for the stuff that takes your full concentration but use those less than perfect moments for all the other writing you've got to do. Newsletters to your mailing list, blog posts, queries, pitches, synopses, and so so many emails... it takes a lot of words to grow a writing life, and you'll need to find time to get them all down sometime!

Experiment. Be flexible. But remember that nothing is a one size fits all solution.

Write when you're not inspired

I said this before. I'll say it again. The real secret to finding more time to write is getting used to writing when you are not inspired. When conditions are less than ideal, when it's an absolute uphill slog, and when you want to quit, you write anyway, or you will never get it done.

One of the biggest reasons most of us feel like we don't have enough writing time is because our definition of writing time is too narrow. When you start stepping out of your comfort zone, your comfort zone itself expands. If you don't limit when you can write, you don't limit what you can do.

Write when you aren't inspired. Write when conditions are less than ideal. It's the only way you'll ever get anything done.

Make the most of the writing time you have

Before I had kids, I had a flexible schedule and plenty of time to write. It wasn't uncommon for me to block myself out four whole uninterrupted hours for writing in glorious daylight when I was wide awake and at my best. Now, I'm booked solid. I only have an hour or two here or there to write and almost always in the dead of night when I'm exhausted and barely coherent. Does it surprise you that I write four times as much now, even though I have a fraction of the time? I have the data to prove it. I write much more now with less time than I ever did when I had all the time in the world.

Thing is, sometimes you think you need more writing time when what you really need is to do more with the time you have. I write more now because I got smarter about how I use my time. I stopped wasting time and started to make the most of what I had.

Let's talk about some ways to do that...

Block distractions

There are a lot of things screaming for your attention, and while sometimes these are literal children you should go keep an eye on, many are notifications and alerts you could safely ignore. It would be nice if we all had the self-control to just NOT look at distracting stuff and get down to work but, alas, it's not that simple. But if you don't want to waste your precious writing time on procrastination and distractions, you've got to block them.

We've all got our vices and, whether it's social media, the news or that fan comic where Mickey and Minnie are vampires, but you'll have to tune it out if you want to get anything done. One of the simplest ways of blocking out all the noise is to shut off the internet on your computer or wifi and data on your phone. While you're at it, take the landline off the hook, unplug the doorbell, and lock your office door. If you're off the grid, no one can bother you!

But it's often not realistic to cut yourself off from the world entirely. Luckily, some apps block just the distracting bits of life while still leaving you available in case of an emergency. Many writers swear by Freedom, a paid app that blocks the internet for as long as you specify. I prefer the free browser extensions LeechBlock and StayFocusd that let me block or even just limit specific sites that I know are distracting while still giving me access the to parts of the web I need (such as the thesaurus, encyclopedia or my banking site for emergencies). I also shut off all but essential notifications and pings, so northing's trying to pull my attention from the task at hand.

Did you know that our will power is finite and you can use it up throughout your day? The more distractions you have to fight, the more you use up your will power and the more likely you are to give in. Make it easier on yourself by limiting the number of things that can pull your attention away from your writing, and you'll be able to make better use of the writing time you do have.

Guard your time

Writing time is significant to you. Block it out on your calendar. Keep it sacred.

No interruptions or preempts! That means no doctor appointments, no coffee dates, and no unexpected visitors. Nothing encroaches on this sacred slot. This is your non-negotiable time to work towards your goals, and you need to be very picky about what you prioritize above it.

At first, the people in your life may not be understanding about this, but they will get it when you are firm that this time is for writing and nothing else. Guarding your writing time makes it feel more significant so you'll be more likely to treat it at such. It also makes it easier to write knowing you won't be interrupted.

Embrace the simple power of saying, "I'm not available." No one needs to know what you are doing, so you don't need to out yourself as a writer if you aren't comfortable doing so. It's none of their business what you use that time for. And playing coy makes it feel like you are doing something cool and illicit, like you've become a spy instead of a newbie writer.

If you want to keep writing in your life, you need to always be actively protecting the space you've made for it.

Go in with a plan

One of the easiest things you can do to make better use of the time you have is to plan out what you will be working on ahead of time. It's incredible how long you can waste floundering around trying to figure out which scene you need to work on or where you left off. Instead, at the end of each writing session, leave yourself a note about what you should work on next so then you'll be able to sit down and get right to it with no delay. This can be as simple as a hint about the next scene or as complicated as a list of things to research or small revisions to make.

Having Past You point Present You in the right writing direction helps make sure you're focused correctly. It also makes it that much easier to get your writing done because you know exactly what to do. This is particularly helpful when you're working early in the morning or late at night. Your tired brain will be very grateful to have a plan that tells it what to work on without having to figure it out. Otherwise, you'll end up working on something random only to realize later that wasn't a priority at all, and now you've wasted that time.

If plotting is your thing, it's also helpful to leave yourself what I think of as a skeleton draft. A skeleton draft is a super shorthand version of the entire scene or section you'll be writing next. It's the bare bones of the whole thing from beginning to end, so you know the general shape when you flesh it out during your next writing session. The less you have to figure out before you write, the more of your writing time you'll be able to use for, well, writing!

If you're not sure what to work on next, the best thing to do is always zoom out and look at the big picture of both your current project and your writing goals. It's easy to get bogged down in the little details day to day, but stepping back and looking at the ultimate destination can help you understand what small step you need to take next to get there.

Your ideal writing circumstances

From curling up with that special pen in the soft chair by the fire to a favorite spot in the coffee shop, your idea writing circumstances are a lot of little things that all add up to making writing more comfortable, familiar and natural. But, by now, you've also realized that you won't always have the luxury of writing in your ideal circumstances. That doesn't mean you can't revel in it when the stars align or that you shouldn't take advantage of those moments when they come because, when you're in your comfort zone, writing is much easier.

What is it about your ideal writing circumstances that makes them work so well for you? What are the essential elements for your ultimate writing comfort? It's a great idea to nail down exactly what you love about your perfect writing situation because then you can replicate it and use it to motivate you when the going gets tough.

Replicate your ideal writing circumstances

Before I had kids, I used to love writing first thing in the morning feeling bright and fresh with a big pot of tea next to me and my favorite tunes blasting through my speakers. Post kids, I'm always writing way too late at night, exhausted from a long day, because it's the only time I have. It's far from my ideal circumstances.

But I've learned that I replicate my ideal circumstances in a lot of little ways to give myself that little extra boost as if I was in my comfort zone. It's about tricking my brain into getting into a focused, writing frame of mind. So while I can't have my usual pot of black tea because of the caffeine, I can make myself a pot of decaf herbal tea. A bright desk light replicates that morning sun I love, and while blasting my tunes is impossible with the kids sleeping next door, I have headphones, so I still get my music. It's not quite what I'd prefer, but it's close enough to get me into the right frame of mind and make writing as painless as possible.

Maybe it's playing background noise of a cafe in your earbuds so you feel like you're at your favorite table at Starbucks instead of on the bus to work. A candle that smells like the garden you'd much rather be writing in. Noise-canceling headphones, so you feel alone instead of listening to your grandfather's TV blaring from the next room. I've even given myself a pretend writing retreat by throwing a YouTube video of a babbling brook up on the TV, sitting on a blanket on the floor and writing in a notebook as if I was really there. It seems silly, and sometimes even feels it, but your brain is surprisingly easy to trick to get into a productive mood with a few cues to remind it of what it prefers.

You can't always write in your ideal circumstances. But when you replicate your most productive environment, sometimes that's enough to help you get focused and down to writing no matter where you are or what's going on around you.

Settling In

There is something so wonderful about being in your own home, a world you made comfortable with your hands. But homeownership is not without its headaches, its leaky roofs and termite infestations, unexpected expenses and back-breaking repairs. It requires maintenance, often messy and sweaty, to keep together, but it's worth it for those moments when you can relax in your own space.

The writing life is not always easy either. Some days are a slog, and it's a struggle to motivate yourself to continue the uphill climb. Really doing it, day in and day out, has a way of divesting you of whatever fantasies you had about what writing would be like.

Turns out, sometimes writing is hard. It's work. It's not even a little fun.

But I would hope that by now you know that it is still worth it. That even if writing is not as joyful and effortless as you may have thought it was, it is in some ways even more magical, the highs sweeter because of the lows. If it were easy, after all, everyone would do it.

Experiment. Learn and grow. Your writing process is the summation of everything that makes you comfortable and thriving within your writing life. While it will always evolve and change as you develop as a writer, paying attention to what works for you helps you work towards your writing goals with a minimum amount of resistance. And just as no two people would decorate a house the same way, it's the very personal and individual nature of your writing process that makes it unique to you.

In this section, you discovered your writing process by...

- Test all writing advice against what you already know works for you.

- Considered the common threads in your writing, the comfort of writing within your literary wheelhouse and the thrill of branching out.
- Found your preferred place to write, either a designated space in your home or a public venue that made you feel productive or inspired.
- Examined the ways you prefer to craft a story from meticulous planning to chasing an idea without a plan.
- Sought out writing buddies to see if you write better alone or with the support of friends.
- Found time to write by auditing your day and identifying your ideal writing time.
- Made time to write by sacrificing, delegating, and thinking outside the text box to alternate ways of writing such as dictation or voice to text.
- Used the little moments and harnessed the power of word sprints for tiny but productive bursts of only a few minutes.
- Scheduled your time knowing some types of writing are better suited some moments than others.
- Wrote when you weren't inspired, no matter how tired you were or how much you didn't feel like it, because you knew it's the only way to reach your writing goals.
- Made the most of your writing time by blocking distractions, guarding your time and going into each writing session with a plan.
- Replicated your ideal writing circumstances to trick your brain into being productive even when conditions were less than perfect.

It's getting real now, isn't it? You have developed not only a writing habit but also your own personal habits of how you prefer to write and what you know works best for you. You have built yourself a writing life in the very middle of your life, so it's time to go live in it!

LIVING THE WRITING LIFE

Look around you. Not bad, is it? Where there was nothing, you have built something, something solid and sturdy that you can live in. You've built yourself a writing life. You started writing and writing regularly, and now it is up to you what to do with it.

Will you build an income and career in novels and movies? Arrange words into art like poetry or find the magic and healing in your own life through memoir? Uncover facts about the world around you and share your skills in articles and other non-fiction writing? Write your way to a greater understanding in meditative journaling or travel to familiar worlds through fan fiction? Or will you do something the world has never seen, weaving unique magic with words no one's yet imagined?

You need not choose now or ever. You may do a bit of each at some point. You make a writing life with words, all of them, words of every kind and genre. You build it with stories, real and imagined, and hold it together with sentences both practical and beautiful, simple and complex. It is facts and fantasy, work and wonder. The writing life is not the telling of just one story but a world of words you construct with the power of your imagination.

A writing life is what you make of it and what you make with it. You can change the world with your words. You can change yourself. Stories are powerful, and you have only begun to wield their magic. This is your chance to do amazing things.

You are truly a writer now, at last. So, what are you waiting for? Get out there and write.

After all, that's what writers do.

ABOUT THE AUTHOR

Hillary DePiano is a playwright, fiction and non-fiction author best known for fantastically funny fairy tales, surprisingly sweet slapstick and unrelentingly upbeat writing advice. With over two dozen plays for everyone from pre-schoolers and up, she's been honored to have her work performed in schools and theatres around the world.

As the author of the *How to Start Writing* series, she regularly shares advice and pep as a blogger and speaker. Since 2010, Hillary heads the Northeastern New Jersey region for NaNoWriMo.org and works as a volunteer in support of their creative mission. She also writes about eBay, e-commerce, and selling online under the name T. W. Seller (TheWhineSeller.com).

For more information about her books, plays, and blogs or to connect via social media, visit HillaryDePiano.com.

Also by Hillary DePiano

Selected Fiction

The Love of Three Oranges
The Green Bird
The Fourth Orange and Other Fairy Tales You've Never
Even Heard Of
Daddy Issues
Polar Twilight
New Year's Thieve
Weak Days
The Author

Non-Fiction

Building a Writing Life
Make Ready to Write!
NaNo What Now?

Writing as T. W. Seller
(TheWhineSeller.com)

Sell Their Stuff
eBay Marketing Makeover
Beyond Amazon, eBay, and Etsy
The Seller Ledger

Printed in the USA
CPSIA information can be obtained
at www.ICGtesting.com
JSHW010109130923
48053JS00010B/133